WILDCATS

WILDCATS

THE STORY OF MILLER CITY'S UNBEATEN STATE CHAMPIONSHIP TEAM OF 1950

DAVE HANNEMAN

TATE PUBLISHING *& Enterprises*

TATE PUBLISHING
& Enterprises

Book design copyright © 2006 by Tate Publishing, LLC. All rights reserved.
Cover design by Lindsay B. Behrens
Interior design by Chris Webb

Published in the United States of America

ISBN: 1–5988655-7-9
06.11.30

ACKNOWLEDGEMENT

A special thanks to Dan Kern, whose diligent and determined research provided a statistical foundation for this book; to Deb, Cody and Sam for being my inspiration; and to Joe Lammers and the Miller City Mighty Mites, who during the 1949–50 season gave basketball fans everywhere proof that miracles can and do happen.

INTRODUCTION

They came from places like Waterloo and Barberton and had wondrous, mystical names like the Wonders and the Magic.

Every year, prep basketball teams from the inner city asphalt to the suburban playgrounds to the small-town barn-ballers fan the flames of basketball fanaticism.

For many fans, the benchmark of Ohio prep basketball was the Waterloo Wonders, one of the most storied teams in Ohio high school history. Coached by the majestically named Magellan E. Hairston, Waterloo raced through the 1933–34 season unbeaten, going 29–0 and winning the Class B state championship.

A year later, after a barn-storming 52–3 season in which the Wonders pulled in huge crowds because of their Globetrotter-like style of play, Waterloo captured a second straight state title.

What is it about small schools who achieve great success that endears us so much to them and their cause? Perhaps it is the symbolism they represent; the American Dream symbolism that if you remain diligent, work hard, stay determined and reach and stretch a bit higher than the other guy you can attain heights you never thought possible.

The Waterloo Wonders became legendary for their exploits so many years ago. But Ohio high school basketball history is filled with teams who have carved a historical niche of their own. This is the story of one of those teams.

Miller City staged its own version of the Waterloo Wonders in 1950, completing a 29–0 season and winning the Class B state championship with a team that included nearly half the male enrollment of the high school.

The small town of Miller City, located in the mid-northern section of Putnam County, boasted roughly 170 residents at the time. There were less than 70 students in the entire high school.

The team's uniforms were six-year-old, faded hand-me-downs from years before.

Their coach was in his first year, fresh out of college. And the team practiced and played its games in a building referred to simply as "The Barn." The floor measured 35 feet by 55 feet and was heated in the winter by pot-bellied stoves in two of the corners.

There was just one locker room. The visitors got that. The home team dressed in a classroom in the school, then ran through the snow and cold to the tiny gymnasium.

But the little team from that tiny town made something wondrous happen during that magical 1949–50 basketball season.

Four years before Milan defeated Muncie in an Indiana state tournament game that gave rise to the movie *Hoosiers* and redefined our current perception of the "Cinderella story," a rag-tag team from a nondescript town in the rich farm lands of Northwest Ohio caught magic in a bottle and made history.

Miller City's run to the 1950 Class B state championship remains one of the great Cinderella stories in Ohio basketball history. And in capturing the hearts and hopes of fans all across the state, a small band of underdogs and a bold young coach emphatically proved you should never let anybody say, "You can't."

A single bead broke away from the sweat herd gathering on C. Norris Simpson's forehead, sped down the crest of his nose and plopped into a darkening spot on his tie.

His new tie. It went with the new suit he'd gotten just that spring when he graduated from Findlay College. The new suit he'd worn that day to make a good first impression on the superintendent of a little school in the rural heartland of Northwest Ohio.

His suit—like his expectations—had been pressed and detailed that morning when he headed out into the August heat. He'd driven west down State Route 224, into and through Ottawa, then north on 108 to the little bug-spot on the map called Miller City.

Findlay was considered small-town by measurable standards at the time. But his home town now seemed metropolitan as Simpson drove past field after field of corn and beans and pastures where milk cows sagged under the summer heat and tail-swatted the flies that incessantly swarmed overhead.

Occasionally, the roof of a house or barn would appear over the crops. But they were few and far between in a farm-belt area where neighbors are measured not by the yard, but by the mile.

Simpson's thoughts suddenly riveted on the small town that rose in the front of him.

"Cross the tracks," he muttered to himself as he went over the directions he'd memorized. "Then take a right."

Superintendent F.M. "Ferd" Ball, a smallish, graying man, was at the school to greet Simpson when he pulled into the parking lot.

"You must be Mr. Simpson," Ball said, extending a hand. "Come, let me give you a quick tour."

Inside the school, their footsteps echoed off shiny tiled floors and resounded through the halls as they passed one empty classroom—"You'll be teaching history there," Ball was saying—after another—"And Social Studies there in 102."

Fresh-scrubbed, smiling faces looked down on them as they passed.

"That the glee club?" Simpson wondered aloud as they passed one picture containing seven young women and three men.

"Nope," Ball answered. "Class of '39."

"Well, how many boys does the school have," Simpson posed.

"I think we have 36 or 37 coming back," Ball answered.

"For basketball?"

"Nope. Whole school."

Simpson nearly bit back the next question on his mind. But the way things were going, he though he'd better ask anyway.

"As far as a staff, are there any assistants coming back?

"Well, you'll be the handling the varsity . . ." Ball said.

"Yeah?"

" . . . and the JV . . ."

"Both teams?"

" . . . and the junior high. You have to realize we're a small school with a small budget."

They were just walking out a side door when Ball's words and a blast-furnace wind hit Simpson in the face like a molten hammer.

"I suppose you'd like to see the gym now," Ball said to the school's new coach.

With that, he headed toward a low-slung, grayish building that Simpson had at first mistaken for a run-down bus garage. But when Ball heaved open the doors, Simpson saw through the half-light that there was indeed a basketball floor inside.

It was, however, unlike any basketball court he'd ever seen.

For starters, it was roughly two-thirds the size of the courts he'd played on at Findlay High School and then Findlay College.

A narrow balcony went around the floor, so close that in the four corners of the court, Simpson, who stood 6-foot-5, could stand inbounds, reach over his head, and grab the beams that supported it.

The August heat wave made the inside of the gymnasium feel like an oven. Come basketball season, Simpson theorized, the same effect would be produced by the two pot-bellied stoves that stood in opposite corners.

"Where's our locker room?" Simpson asked.

The answer came back slowly, almost evasively.

"Well," the superintendent drawled, "our kids usually change over in the school, in the typing room, then run over here to the gym. There's only one locker room here, you know, and that's for the visiting team," Ball added, opening the door to a room under the bleachers that a skinny midget would have called cramped.

The tour over, they headed back out into the boiling sun and the blazing heat and the simmering future.

"School starts in two weeks. See you then," Ball said as they shook hands one last time.

Then Simpson slid behind the wheel and pointed his car toward home. But at the edge of the parking lot, he stopped, mulling over a day that had seemed to drag on forever but was suddenly over.

Three months ago he was a student. Now they wanted him to teach.

Six months ago he was a player. Now they wanted him to coach.

Simpson turned and looked at the small school and the slab gray building that was its gymnasium. What was it Ball had said? Something about the building being called "The Barn," and how it was supposedly built some years back by the school's industrial arts class.

Simpson turned back, muttering as he headed down the road as the hot August sun beat down and the sweat beaded on his forehead, slid down his nose and plopped onto his tie.

"Charlie, my boy," he said to himself. "Just what the heck have you gotten yourself into?"

Skip knew.

Skip knew, and Joe Lammers knew that he knew.

Joe shouldn't have been surprised. Ralph "Skip" Meyer was his best friend and closest confidant. They'd grown up together, not only neighbors but cousins as well.

They started shooting hoops on the New Cleveland School playground way back in first-grade and never looked back. A binding friendship had been forged during blazing summers and frigid winters and those long, long rides with Fr. Schmelzer, side by side in the back seat of his car, praying the rosary on another road trip to another CYO tournament.

Closer than brothers, they'd shared all the highs and lows two young men could share, from games won and love lost to their most well-guarded hopes and dreams.

That's why the sullen silence was now so unbearable.

It was a chilly October Friday afternoon, and a steady rain was pelting the brittle brown corn stalks that rustled in the breeze. But as the two boys drove home from school, there was none of the usual banter of crops to harvest and everyday chores and the one pure thing that had dominated much of their lives up to then—the upcoming basketball season.

Something was wrong. And Skip knew it.

"Spill it Joe. What's bugging you?"

Joe thought about wrapping himself in silence. The problem was his alone, and silence would be the armor that kept prying eyes away.

But the words were out of his mouth before he could contain them, and once they started, they wouldn't stop.

"Skip, I've been thinking about quitting."

"What? School?"

"No, you doof. Basketball."

"Basketball? You're kidding me!"

"I've just been thinking about it, Skip."

"But you and me have been playing ball since forever, Joe. We're seniors. We're lettermen. This is our last year of high school ball. You can't be serious."

"I don't know Skip. Something's just different this year."

"What is it? The new coach? You still bummed because he kicked you out of practice when you didn't want to do calisthenics the other day?"

"Maybe that's part of it, Skip. Geez, we open the season in a couple of weeks, and what have we done to get ready? Run. That's it. Run, run and run some more. If I wanted to go through boot camp, I'd join the Army.

"You know, Nienberg may not have been the greatest coach we ever had. But he got us to the district finals a couple of years ago, and he at least had us running an offense and a defense. This new guy, Simpson, does a lot of hollerin.' But I swear he's going to run us into the ground before we ever play our first game."

For one of the few times in all the years he'd known him, Joe saw Skip go completely quiet. But as he pulled into the Lammers' driveway, Skip offered one parting bit of advice.

"Joe, think hard about what you're doing. You know what basketball's meant to you and me over the years. You, me, Junior, Dick, Frank, Vern, Roy—we can be a pretty decent team this year. Don't give that all up yet. Think about it over the weekend. I'll see ya Monday, okay?"

Saturday dawned crisp and clear. And after his morning chores, Joe Lammers did what he often did to kill a few idle hours; he shot some hoops. Right baseline, right wing, across the top of the key, left wing, left baseline. There was something calming in shooting baskets, something soothing in the set, stroke and swish of the ball finding the bottom of the net.

Friday's conversation with Skip hadn't dispersed the gnawing doubt in his gut. But getting it out in the open would force the issue. He'd thrown down a gauntlet, a challenge to himself if no one else.

Monday would be here before he knew it. It would be one long, interesting weekend.

Norris Simpson was wondering if his students despised Monday mornings as much as he did. But one look at his first period history class, hunched nervously over their midterm exams, pretty much confirmed his suspicions.

Simpson could relate. It hadn't been that many months since he'd been a student himself, finishing up his final year at Findlay College. Then, degree in hand, he went looking for a job.

His future, he knew, was uncertain. But he was sure of two things: One, he liked teaching. And two, he wanted to coach basketball.

Basketball had been a cornerstone in his life for as long as he could remember. He was never the best athlete on the team. But he became a student of the game, worked hard on his skills and was as fundamentally sound as they came. That dedication and a high-school growth spurt that saw him sprout up to almost 6-foot-4 served him well. He lettered three years at Findlay High and started his junior and senior seasons.

His senior year was a memorable one for Simpson and his teammates. Under the masterful tutelage of head coach Carl Bachman, a man Simpson grew to respect and admire as much as any mentor during his career, the Trojans went 16–0 during the regular season, clinching an undisputed Buckeye League championship when Simpson, with three starters on the bench after fouling out, came through with 11 key points in a 49–47 win over Fremont.

Findlay then rattled off four more wins before falling to Toledo Woodward in the Class A (big school) regional semifinals. The regional was played at Bowling Green State University, which had recently installed those new see-through glass backboards, something neither Findlay nor Woodward had seen before. But Bachman, ever the innovator, requested that they be painted white so neither team would be at an unfamiliar disadvantage.

Tournament officials complied. Sadly, the change did not work for the Trojans, whose season ended with a 46–38 loss in the Sweet Sixteen.

Simpson's first college of choice was Miami of Ohio. But he never felt he fit in there, and soon returned home. Now a lanky 6-foot-5, Simpson continued his basketball career at Findlay College where another of his mentors, Don Renninger, molded him not only as a player but as a future coach as well.

"Uh, Mr. Simpson?"

The voice pulling Simpson back from his daydream down memory lane belonged to Roy Meyer, a sophomore on the basketball team.

"Mr. Simpson, can I sharpen my pencil?"

"Sure, Roy. Go ahead."

Simpson liked Meyer. Energetic and easy-going, he had a quiet confidence about him. He also had a pair of the quickest hands he'd ever seen on a basketball player and a first step to the basket that was a blur.

Roy Meyer had been a pleasant surprise when Simpson opened

basketball practice two weeks earlier. But the first-year coach was finding a number of pleasant surprises at this little back roads school in the heart of Putnam County.

Simpson had had his doubts when he was offered the basketball job at Miller City. He'd seen the name of the school in the local paper a few times. He figured it was just another of the small burgs from Putnam County, where the three basic fundamentals of life were farming, religion and basketball, and not necessarily in that order.

His first impressions left him slightly stunned. He'd had more kids in his graduating class at Findlay High School than Miller City, population 170, had in the entire town. He'd had as many kids in some of his classes as they had in the whole high school.

Simpson had been especially shocked by the gymnasium, a term used rather loosely for the facility where the Wildcats would practice and play their games. The town's old-timers recollected it had been built sometime in the early '20s by the school's industrial arts class. Low-slung, the building's ceiling was 18 feet high at the peak. The small floor was more a stage than a basketball court, but at least it was solid. As Simpson heard it, a player was driving for a lay-up a season or two ago when he planted his foot and broke straight through the brittle boards. So the school had the old floor replaced, with the players, Simpson learned, going door-to-door soliciting donations to cover the cost of the materials.

Two rows of plank bleachers ran the length of the building, but many fans preferred to stand. In the corners, that meant the tips of their shoes were sometimes right on the court, an interesting dilemma for both the home team and the opposition.

Appropriately dubbed "The Barn," the building had just one small locker room and was heated by two pot-bellied stoves that had branded many a player, home team and visitor alike, who dared make a mad dash into the corner to retrieve a loose ball.

As September slipped into October, Simpson had gone about lining things up for practice. One of the first things he discovered was that the school owned just two basketballs and one of them was a laced-up model from a bygone era. He'd requested more from Superintendent Ball and got a quick response—"Sure, if you have the money for 'em."

The varsity uniforms were in sorry condition as well. There were two sets—yellow ones for homes games, blue ones for when the Wildcats were on the road.

Simpson immediately ditched the tattered and torn blue uniforms. At one time, they might have had a brilliant luster. Now they were mostly off-gray and falling apart.

The yellow jerseys were slightly better. If need be, the Wildcats would wear them, home and away, all season long. New uniforms would have been best. But that was not an option because, as Superintendent Ball said, "That money went for the new band uniforms. We'll see about fixing the basketball team up next year."

Warm-ups? The players had to provide their own, as well as their shoes and socks.

It was not what Simpson had envisioned when he set out to be a teacher and coach. But Charles and Zina Simpson had not raised their boy to be a whiner, a quitter or a pessimist. He'd been hired to teach English and history and coach basketball, and, to the best of his ability, that was what he intended to do. He'd never shirked a responsibility before, and he didn't plan on starting now.

Ever the optimist, Simpson had a strong belief in himself and his methods. The obstacles before him were just new challenges to be faced and cleared.

He also had a tenuous faith in his players. They seemed a motley bunch at first. The only player with much size was a senior named Dick Barlage. He stood a bit over 6–1 and tipped the scales at around 235. But he was immoveable around the basket, positioned himself well, and had a little half-hook shot that was impossible to stop.

Simpson had a couple of senior forwards—one a tad over 6-foot, the other just under—named Ralph Meyer and Joe Lammers.

Meyer, who went by 'Skip,' and Lammers seemed inseparable on and off the court. Both were excellent shots, though he felt that, at times, they relied on the long set shots a bit too often.

The guards were small, both 5–6 or 5–7, but very quick. The senior—Frank Schroeder—was a proven leader who could score and get after it on defense; a sophomore—nicknamed 'Junior' McDonald, ironically—was a slashing left-hander who could beat just about any defender off the dribble.

Simpson already knew that those five would see a lot of playing time, along with Mel Lammers, another senior, and Karl Inkrott, the only junior on the roster.

To Simpson, they were all just names on the morning roll when classes started in September. But he'd seen something more in his first few months at the school. Many days he spent his lunch break leaning against the school building, basking in the autumn sunshine as the students enjoyed their precious few minutes of freedom before heading into the school for afternoon classes.

Invariably a basketball would appear, as if by magic, and a pickup game would break out. Every kid on the playground, it seemed, could shoot the ball—the obvious result of long hours spent practicing on hoops and rusty rims on the garages and in the haymows. Simpson saw on every homestead he passed on his way to and from the school.

He noticed something else as well, an almost effortless poetic symmetry to the way they set picks and screens and set up an offensive flow, a clean confidence to the way they worked the ball. When these kids played ball, there was none of the sloppy carelessness of the uncaring or the unconcerned.

These kids knew the game. They knew and understood the subtle intricacies of basketball like a thousand other kids who had spent uncounted hours challenging each other and themselves to succeed at the simple chore of throwing a ball through a hoop.

Simpson saw potential on that playground. But he knew potential meant nothing without results, and as the chilling winds signaled the fast approach of the first days of practice, he thought long and hard about how he could mold that potential into a winner.

He knew he'd have problems. There were only 37 boys in the entire high school; a little over half came out for basketball, and of that number he counted seven, maybe eight, he felt could contribute night in and night out.

And, by varsity standards, they were small. Man, were they ever. Simpson had played on junior high teams with as much physical size as this Miller City bunch. Guards 5–6 and 5–7. Forwards barely reaching 6-foot. A chunky center who stood out as much for his width as his height.

Those were factors Simpson had no control over. So he focused on the positives instead—quickness, an uncanny shooting ability, and an almost psychic sixth sense of their teammates' movements on the floor.

Day after day, on his drive to and from his little apartment in Ottawa, Simpson plotted and planned. And as he drove he saw his players, either early in the morning or right after school, changed into their work clothes and heading for the barn. This was farm country, and in farm country there were always chores to do.

That might have been the spark for his plan. Physically, Simpson knew his Wildcats wouldn't match up well with many teams on the schedule. But if he could get his players to outwork and outhustle the other team, they might just win a few games.

Farm kids were used to hard work. Simpson's idea was to get them to work as hard at their game as they did their chores. And when practice officially started in early October, that's exactly what he did, working his players like they'd never been worked before, not on the basketball court anyway.

It was a gamble. And Simpson knew he might meet with some resistance.

He was right.

At the very first practice, Joe Lammers, one of the key players he was sorely counting on, sat down in the middle of a workout and refused to go on.

"We never had to do all this running and stuff when Coach Nienberg was here," Lammers groused as he stood up and headed for the door.

Simpson had heard all about Joe Nienberg, the man he replaced. Good coach. Nice guy. But some thought he'd been a bit too easy on the previous teams. Miller City had been in the thick of things the previous two years. But back-to-back 8–3 records in the tough Putnam County League left them just shy of the title, and a year ago, Leipsic had knocked them out of the tournament in the district finals.

Simpson knew he couldn't afford to lose Lammers—a senior, a returning starter and one of the best shots on the team. But he also knew that if he was going to coach that team, he needed total control and full commitment. So he sent Charlie Warnimont, a freshman manager for the team, after Lammers to convey that very message.

Lammers returned to practice the next day, and did all that was asked of him. But Simpson sensed that two hard weeks of strenuous training hadn't softened Lammers' disposition towards him. He was afraid he still might lose him, especially after last Friday's practice. Lammers hadn't even looked at him when he and Skip Meyer left the gym that day. Lammers was stewing inside, battling his emotions, and Simpson knew it.

Simpson hoped he would stick it out. They were close, so very close. The two weeks of training and drills had molded the team into a lean (except for the Barlage boy), hungry group that could scrap and scramble with the best of them. They were ready to take the next step in his plan, but he needed every ounce of talent and experience that the little school could provide.

Suddenly, the bell rang, ending first period and, for the second time that day, rousing Simpson from his daydream. As the students filed out, they placed their history tests on Simpson's desk.

Roy Meyer was one of the last one's out the door.

"See ya at practice, coach," he called.

"I'll be there," Simpson sighed. "I'll be there."

Norris Simpson paced the floor liked an expectant father.

Figuratively, that's what he was.

Dressed in a light tan suit with a melon-green shirt, an outfit that would become a superstitious trademark of his throughout the season, Simpson huddled with his players in the Miller City High School typing room that doubled as the Wildcats' locker room on game nights.

Opening night, his first as a head coach, was 20 minutes away, and it was hard to discern who was more nervous, him or his young players.

Just getting this far with his entire team intact was a small victory in itself, Simpson thought. There had been some tough times.

He knew he had alienated some players with what they considered a drill sergeant approach and a heavy emphasis on conditioning. Heck, as recently as two weeks ago, he was afraid he might have lost one of his best players, a senior forward named Joe Lammers.

He remembered that Monday vividly. After a long day of mid-term exams, he'd seen the boys head home for their evening chores. He recalled wondering if they'd all be back for the 7 p.m. practice.

That's why he paid extra attention that night as the headlights pulled into the parking lot and the players started showing up. Frank Schroeder, one of his senior captains, and his brother Vern were the first to arrive; then Dick Barlage, his big guy in the middle; Junior McDonald, a talented sophomore guard Simpson was always getting on; and Karl Inkrott, who would also see some time inside for the Wildcats.

Finally, piling out of the last car with gym bags in hand, were Skip Meyer and his younger brother, Roy, followed by the Lammers brothers, Joe and Mel.

"Good to see you, Joe," Simpson said as they filed past him and headed for the locker room.

Joe just nodded.

Simpson still looked on that night as a pivotal turning point. For the first time since they had started getting ready for the 1949–50 season, Simpson opened practice not with the usual calisthenics, but with a short talk. He explained his reasoning for drilling the team as he had, emphasizing that he wanted the best-conditioned team possible to run the kind of offense and defense he felt the Wildcats needed to employ if they were to have any chance against teams bigger or stronger than them.

Then they practiced, and it was unlike any practice they'd been through before. Simpson was as vocal as ever, but now there were strict directions on exactly what he wanted them to execute on each end of the floor.

Offensively, Simpson was counting heavily on the heady leadership and scoring talents of play-making senior guard Frank Schroeder, the slashing style of sophomore guard Junior McDonald and the deadly outside shooting and baseline play of senior forwards Skip Meyer and Joe Lammers. The post position was an uncertainty, but in big Dick Barlage and Vern Schroeder, a sophomore, Simpson felt he had some material to work with.

Defensively, Simpson favored a 2–3 zone, with his guards harassing the other teams' playmakers and his front-liners forming a basic triangle inside, the better to screen out opposing rebounders and hopefully negate Miller City's lack of size.

Simpson threw in some new wrinkles as well, like a full-court press, a tactic the Wildcats had rarely used before. He also stressed a transition game. Both were designed to best utilize the talent he had available. The press, Simpson figured, would wear down bigger teams, and the transition game would allow his Wildcats to be on the attack before the opposition could set up on defense.

If Simpson had any doubts about his blueprint, they were quickly erased. The players loved his style, relishing the freedom it gave them to create opportunities on the fly. Besides, the basic fundamentals of the system—playing good defense, grabbing a rebound or forcing a turnover, and pressing the attack on offense—fit well with the style they had grown up playing in their own haymows and driveways.

It worked well in practice. But would it work under game conditions?

Simpson found out soon enough. About a week before the season opened, he approached Carl Bachman, his former coach at Findlay High, and asked if he could bring his Wildcats over for a scrimmage.

Bachman obliged.

Simpson was well aware of the challenge. Findlay was one of the biggest schools in Northwest Ohio and had a strong basketball tradition. Just two years before, Bachman had led them to the Class A state championship.

But the Wildcats quickly verified Simpson's faith in them, and in himself. Miller City not only stayed with the Trojans, but won their share of possessions. They had passed their first test.

Now it was time to open their show for real. No more scrimmages where you could blow your whistle, stop everyone in their tracks and start all over. Now every game ended with a "W" or an "L" that went into a ledger and remained a part of the team's—and the school's—history.

Miller City opened the 1949–50 season at home against Continental. Long-time Putnam County basketball aficionados would tell you Continental was a team to contend with that season, a solid team as usual, and not to be taken lightly.

Pacing the typing room turned locker room, Simpson sensed the pre-game tension of his team. He knew the feeling, the gut-tightening knot that formed in the pit of your stomach and sat there like a rock. In high school, Coach Bachman called them opening night jitters. He had a novel way of dealing with them, telling jokes, usually with a little green frog as the central character.

If it was good enough for the master . . . , Simpson thought.

"Two frogs are sitting on a lily pad," Simpson began as he eyed his young players. But his mind suddenly went blank. He couldn't remember the rest of the joke. Not even the punch line.

Not that it mattered. Just then, there was a knock on the door, and Charlie Warnimont poked his head into the room.

"Uh, they're about ready to start coach," he said. "You ready?"

"As ready as we'll ever be, I guess," Simpson answered as they headed out into the night, jackets and overcoats shouldered against the chill November night.

As the team approached "The Barn," they could hear muffled sounds coming from inside. Then the doors were flung open, and they were engulfed by the warm inside air and the blare of the pep band as it signaled their arrival.

The stands were packed with fans looking to get their first glimpse of the new coach and his team, packed being an insufficient word for a building that, at most, could seat maybe 150 people. The two rows of plank boards lining one side of the building were full, and the rest, home towns fans and visitors alike, stood three and four deep in the corners and even spilled onto the floor.

Simpson put his players through their pre-game warm-ups, noticing just a bit of a nervous flush whenever they glanced into the crowd and caught a glimpse of a parent or a friend, maybe even a sweetheart up in the stands.

At that time as much as any other, Simpson knew why he so loved this game they called basketball, why people would leave their cozy homes on cold winter nights to cram themselves hip to hip into tiny gymnasiums to watch young men—boys really—run and jump and throw a leather ball through a round metal hoop.

It was, in essence, just a game. But it had a power to pull communities together in a rare, supportive way. People would always disagree on everything from politics to planting time. But to root for the home town team on game night was as bonding as marriage and just as serious.

When the horn sounded, Simpson herded his players to the bench. The pep band belted out a rousing rendition of the Star Spangled Banner, Simpson delivered a few final instructions and then it was time to begin a new season for his players, a new career for him.

Simpson had worried that his players might be tentative. But he saw none of the earlier nervousness as the Wildcats surged to a 12–4 first-quarter lead. Opening at home was an obvious plus for Miller City. Continental had trouble finding any rhythm, struggling, it seemed, with the confines of the court and the Wildcats' scrappy, aggressive defense.

Miller City nursed its lead through the half, survived a third-quarter rally that saw Continental close the gap to 28–21, then milked out a 37–34 victory.

Simpson had been up and down off the bench the entire game, exhorting his players to move the ball better on offense, to box out on the boards, to work it, work it, work it on defense.

He knew the game was not a work of art, not by his standards anyway. But Simpson got just what he wanted and what the team needed from Frank Schroeder, Miller City's senior guard and co-captain. Schroeder had fouled out in the fourth quarter, a direct reflection of his aggressive defensive play. But he'd also scored 17 points and supplied the leadership Simpson was hoping to get from his veterans.

And when it was over, Simpson breathed a heavy sigh of relief as he sank back on the bench and let it all sink in.

Several fans came up to congratulate him on the win, calloused hands pumping his as faces he'd never seen before and names he'd not yet learned filed past.

Later, on the drive back to his apartment in Ottawa, Simpson allowed himself to smile a satisfied smile. It was only Game One of what would be a long, long season. But he was 1–0, and of all the coaches in the entire state of Ohio that night—young, idyllic men like him and time-tested veterans alike—only half of them could say that.

Norris Simpson was smiling, almost giddy, as he climbed into his car and headed out of Ottawa, west toward State Route 108 on the short trip to Miller City. As the rookie head coach of the Wildcats, he'd worked himself and his players hard getting ready for the 1949–50 season. But even his own quiet confidence had not prepared him for the sterling ride his players had given him over the past three weeks.

Simpson never doubted that his system, his style of play, would pay off. He just never expected it to blossom so fast so soon.

There had been that close call in the season opener, a tentative 3-point win over Continental. But a week later, the Wildcats had played Glandorf, and for the first time that season—but certainly not the last—Simpson marveled at what could happen when you catch lightning in a bottle.

Maybe it was the fact that the Wildcats were going against Joe Nienberg, their former coach who had moved on to teach at

Glandorf and coach in that school's new gymnasium. Maybe it was simply the fact that, after weeks of intense practice and preparation, the players had embraced Simpson's system and understood exactly what it was they needed to do. Maybe it was just fate.

Simpson was his usual self in the Glandorf game, often up off the bench to yell out instructions. But a strange thing was happening out on the floor. More often than not, just as Simpson was about to speak, the players beat him to the punch, switching on their own, making subtle adjustments to adapt to the game.

It struck him then, like a beam of sunlight on an overcast day. They knew. They understood. They had it—that certain blend of talent and teamwork and chemistry and effort that he knew was in their veins from the first time he'd seen them playing pickup games on the playground.

It was a wondrous thing to see. The offense flowed, the defense was tenacious, the shots fell and the Glandorf turnovers mounted. When it was over, the Wildcats raced howling off the floor, a convincing 63–26 victory in the books.

Frank Schroeder once again proved his leadership with 18 points. But the Wildcats also showed their balance with Skip Meyer, Joe Lammers and Junior McDonald in doubles figures as well.

If Simpson had any doubts the Glandorf game was a fluke, his players dispelled them a week later when they stampeded their way to another lopsided win, beating Ottawa Public 68–34 in the Putnam County League opener for both schools.

Dick Barlage, inserted into the starting lineup the week before, had a break-out game, dominating inside with that big frame, scoring consistently with that little baseline hook of his and scoring 21 points. Frank Schroeder added 19 points to help offset the absence of Joe Lammers, who missed the game due to a death in the family.

That game not only got the Wildcats off to a good start in PCL play, it also served as a proving ground for a defensive tactic that would become a pivotal tool for the Wildcats. Miller City led

Ottawa just 8–6 after the first quarter and 18–15 at the half. But Simpson ordered a full-court press to start the third quarter and the move paid off big, with Miller City blitzing Ottawa 50–19 in the second half.

The same tactic paid off again a few nights later. In a rematch with Continental, this time on the Pirates' home floor, Miller City appeared sluggish through a see-saw first half. But the press turned the tide once again, this time resulting in an 18–0 third-quarter barrage that broke the game wide open.

Miller City's 4–0 start had people talking, and it wasn't just the home-town fans taking notice. A 66–47 non-league win over Holgate boosted interest even more and stoked the fires for a December 16 showdown with Ottoville, a tall and talented team many felt was the cream of the Putnam County League crop that season.

Inside, Ottoville returned one of the best big men in the league in Gene Schimmoeller. Tom Weber ran the show out front, a heady guard and dangerous if left unguarded.

The Big Green also had a lanky forward that year named Dick Kortokrax. Kortokrax would finish his career at Ottoville, earn his college degree, and return to the Putnam County League where, at Fort Jennings, Ottoville and Kalida, he would amass more wins than any prep coach in Ohio high school basketball history.

The two teams were unbeaten when they squared off, both in league games and overall. Miller City, 5–0 overall and 2–0 in the PCL, was coming off a torrid four-game run in which the Wildcats had averaged almost 60 points a game. Ottoville, also 2–0 in the PCL, was 4–0 on the season.

Despite a packed partisan house at The Barn, Miller City had trouble handling the Big Green right from the start, especially Schimmoeller inside and Weber's deadly accuracy from the wing. The Big Green led 18–11 after the first quarter and nudged their lead to 29–21 by the half.

But the Wildcats battled back, using some tenacious defense

and an offensive surge by Skip Meyer and Barlage to creep within one—39–38—heading into the fourth quarter.

Keeping the pressure on, Miller City finally caught Ottoville and tied the game 41–41, then surged ahead 47–42 on a free throw by Frank Schroeder. Schimmoeller answered for Ottoville, his 15th and 16th points of the night. But the Big Green were forced to foul, and Miller City added another free throw, then rebounded an Ottoville miss and ran out the clock.

The season was still young. There would be many more games in many more gymnasiums before the 1949–50 season would be finally put into the books.

But Miller City's 48–44 win over Ottoville sent a resounding message throughout the league and the surrounding area. These Wildcats were no flash in the pan, one-shot wonders with a couple of key veterans carrying the load and a boisterous rookie head coach calling the shots.

This Miller City team was for real. And in the weeks and months that followed, many more doubting opponents would find that out.

The laughter of unfettered youth rang through the crisp night air as Skip and Roy Meyer pulled into the Lammers' driveway and Joe and Mel piled into the Chevy.

It was Saturday night. Chores were long since divvied up and done. And with no game on the schedule, it was time to do what all young men with boundless energy and a little free time on their hands like to do—get out and howl.

There was a wedding dance in town that night. And the boys, basking in the communal adulation that a winning, unbeaten basketball team can foster, were enjoying their newfound status. There was nodding acknowledgement now whenever they were seen throughout school, in church, around town.

The basketball team had become more than an ice-breaker to casual conversations, edging out the usual topics like new births, unexpected deaths, crop prices and the unseasonable weather.

They had become a community magnet, polarizing the hopeful

expectations of old men and pretty young girls, of proud parents and die-hard basketball fans who dared to dream that these chosen few were invincible. Winter is a bleak season, though, and their expectations were tempered with the cold, hard realization of how threadbare is the thin coat separating the eternal optimism of victories not yet won from the dream-shattering emptiness and finality of defeat.

But young gods tend to be myopic. Why consider the inevitable when the immediate is so full of promise?

They were riding high after knocking off a mighty Ottoville team many considered the best in the area. The next battle was days away, and adoring fans awaited their arrival.

Life was definitely good.

As the boys pushed open the doors, they were immediately embraced by the warmth of the hall and the people in it. Backs were patted and hands were pumped as they made their way through the crowd. Decker's Red Shirts—always a foot-stomping band—was cranking out reels and square dances and getting the crowd wound up.

The boys worked their way to one side of the hall, found an opening along the wall, and turned to scope things out.

Some of their other teammates were already there. Frank Schroeder, whose tenacity and floor leadership were proving to be truly inspiring for the Wildcats, held court at a nearby table, a gaggle of giggling school girls hanging on his every word.

Big Dick Barlage hung near the dessert table, temptation gnawing at him like a winter wind. The boy could put it away, that was for sure. But the Wildcats had been putting away some pretty good opponents because of his immoveable presence in the middle.

Junior McDonald, lightning quick on the court, was a blur off it as well, zipping from one group of laughing teenagers to another.

Karl Inkrott and Jerry Kuhlman sauntered by, stopped to trade a verbal jab or two, then continued on.

When a town has but 170 residents, even something as personal as a wedding reception becomes a community celebration, a gathering of friends and family and acquaintances where those who are formally invited and those who are not go to see and be seen and share.

And in those dying days of 1949, with Christmas looming a few weeks away and an undefeated basketball team boosting everybody's spirits, there was an added golden tinge to the season.

Joe Lammers was the first to notice, across the way, the tall angular man talking to a small but animated group of people.

Their eyes locked for a moment. Then both nodded and turned back to their friends.

"Skip," Joe whispered. "Coach is here."

"Where?"

"Over there, talking with Superintendent Ball and those guys."

Skip's eyes scanned the hall, eventually locating the huddle Joe had first discovered.

"What do ya think he's doing here? Checking up on us?"

"Don't know," Joe said. "Don't know."

The first time Norris Simpson met with his team, he'd outlined his goals for the season. He'd stressed themes like teamwork, hustle and determination. He'd also laid down a set of rules—no drinking, no smoking, hit the books and stay out of trouble.

Basically, they were rules all coaches dictated to their teams every season. Whether all coaches strictly adhered to those rules was debatable. No team, obviously, wanted to lose a key player over what some would deem a petty infraction.

In Simpson's case, he had little to worry about. He had a group of players seemingly unfettered by vices.

Tempted? Certainly. But they were more prone to follow the rules than to challenge authority. Rules were something they had to live by every day, whether they were founded in their religious background or their family upbringing.

It was the way things were. It was the way things needed to be. And they understood that.

Later, on the ride home, Coach Simpson's appearance at the wedding dance was still on the boys' minds.

"Do ya think he was spying on us, Skip," Joe asked.

"Nah. I doubt it." Skip answered.

"But his apartment is clear over in Ottawa. Why'd he come clear over here, and on a night off? Coach Nienberg never did nothin' like that."

"Coach Nienberg never got us off to a 6–0 start, neither," Skip said. "Hey, we're going good. Coach has a great system, the system is working and we're winning ball games.

"Maybe he's just making sure we don't do something stupid to screw it up."

"Skip? How far do you think we can go?"

"Don't know, Joe. Don't know. But if we keep playing the way we're playing, I think we're going to be alright."

Norris Simpson rolled out of bed, scraped the frost from his upstairs bedroom window, and peered out through the glass.

It had gotten cold last night. Bitter cold.

There was no school because of the holiday break, and for one fleeting second, he considered diving back under the inviting warmth of the covers. But Norris Simpson was not one to tempt fate by wasting opportunity, especially when things were going so well.

And things had been going very well for his Miller City basketball team.

Following a pivotal win over a strong Ottoville team, Simpson had harbored a budding concern that his Wildcats might regress. A former player himself and a lifetime student of the game, Simpson had seen firsthand the physical and mental letdown that can follow a huge emotional win.

With only one day to prepare for a December 20 game with

Kalida, Simpson debated whether to run the boys through a relatively easy practice on Monday or to run any overconfidence right out of them.

He decided to do a little of both, interspersing some all-out end-to-end play with frequent breaks in the action, reinforcing at every stop that, yes, beating Ottoville was a definitive plus for the players, the school and the community; but it was just one game in a season of many games, and with each win came a bit more pressure to go out and prove themselves a legitimate contender all over again.

Maybe it was that last statement that did the trick. When Miller City traveled to Kalida for the annual showdown with the other Wildcats in the Putnam County League, it was no battle at all.

Sharp from the get-go, Miller City controlled the game from the opening tip, racing to an early lead and cruising to a 63–29 victory.

Skip and Joe, two of the team's deadliest shooters, were red-hot all night. Skip scored 14 points; Joe had 13. Dick Barlage continued to be a force in the middle with 12 points as Miller City's front court trio accounted for 39 of the team's points.

Two nights later, back on their home floor, the Wildcats lit up Vaughnsville 82–38 in their biggest offensive showing of the season. A good shooting team all along, Miller City put on a clinic in the first eight minutes, racing to a 23–7 lead.

They never looked back.

Skip, Joe and Frank Schroeder—who'd been calling themselves the Three Musketeers since they all started shooting baskets together as first-graders on the New Cleveland School playground—lived up to that nickname by sharing scoring honors, all with 18 points. Junior and Dick added 13 each.

The game was more than an eye-catching blowout in the prep scores in Saturday's papers. It was validation that Simpson's system and Miller City's talent was blending together to form an irrepressible combination.

More than a few opposing coaches took note.

Miller City fans celebrated not only a white Christmas, but an unblemished, undefeated 8–0 basketball team as well. But in the cold, quiet solitude of the Christmas break, Simpson remained on edge. There was another game today, and it would be a game unlike any of the others.

This was the traditional game between the varsity and the alumni. Big brother against little brother. A chance for the men who had graduated on to the real jobs and responsibility of an adult to once again teach the youngsters a lesson or two. This would be their come-uppance, as it had been for years in the driveways and the haymows all over the area where age always seemed to play as big a role as talent in any pick-up game.

Simpson knew none of the alumni players. He'd seen them at games often enough, but as fans in the stands, not as competition in opposing uniforms. He could only control the players in his charge, though, so he wanted to be prepared.

Simpson padded downstairs, cursing John Lewis and his coal strike as he tossed a lump from his dwindling supply into the stove, and fixed a hasty breakfast. He spent the morning going over his meticulously organized notes. By early afternoon, he was cruising out of Ottawa on Route 115, heading toward Route 108 and the straight shot north into Miller City.

When you're the only coach in the entire program and you have three games on the schedule—junior high, JV and varsity—getting to the gym early isn't an option; it's a necessity.

Simpson let himself into "The Barn" and waited while his eyes adjusted to the half-lit gloom inside. Custodian Izzy Noon was already there, stoking the pot-bellied stoves that sat in opposite corners and served as the building's only source of heat.

Simpson was happy when Dick Krauss showed up soon after. Krauss and Simpson had been teammates, first at Findlay High School, later at Findlay College. Simpson had always admired the spunk and court savvy of the little guard, so when he asked Krauss if he wanted to help with the Miller City program, he was elated when his friend jumped at the chance.

Mostly, Krauss scouted upcoming opponents. But with the holiday break and the alumni game being on an off-day—Wednesday instead of the usual Tuesday-Friday schedule—he had decided to come over and join Simpson on the bench.

Simpson and Krauss were reminiscing about old times, like good friends often do, when the players began filing in. Superintendent Ferd Ball was close behind, then some of the volunteers who would take the tickets and run the concession stand.

Gradually, the gymnasium began to fill. Eventually, it was overflowing. It seemed the whole town was there, but that was to be expected for a game like this—where brother was pitted against brother, and parents' allegiances switched possession by possession.

"This game doesn't mean a thing in the league standings," Simpson told his team just before the opening tip. "But any time you take the floor, all I ask is that you to play to win."

In the first few minutes of the game, the varsity seemed a bit tentative. But then the weeks of practice and the experience of tough league battles began to kick in. With Simpson exhorting them from the sidelines, the varsity players found their stride and began to take charge.

Simpson knew his varsity would have an edge in conditioning, and he exploited that edge. Quicker on defense and better in transition, the varsity poured in 46 points in the first half alone and cruised to a 72–45 win.

Skip played a phenomenal game, scoring 26 points. His older brother, who had graduated a few years earlier, led the alumni with 14.

Afterwards, there were the customary congratulations.

"Great team you got there, Coach."

"Keep up the good work."

"You got the boys playing some real solid basketball, Simpson."

It was late when Simpson finally turned the key in the lock and opened the door to his chilly apartment.

One year would soon be over. A new year was about to begin. Linking the two, however, was a basketball season. In a few days, Miller City would take the floor once again. Hamler, a big, physical team, was anxiously waiting for the unbeaten Wildcats to pay a visit to their place.

Simpson wondered, as he warmed his hands by the stove, what their coach and their players were doing right now. It was the Christmas break after all.

Then he switched on the single light over the kitchen table and pulled out his scouting reports.

There was work to do.

The world was in turmoil as 1949 slipped into the history books.

The Cold War was heating up as East and West clashed in a power struggle of ideologies. Russia's Andrei Vishinksi was openly challenging the North Atlantic Pact. Tensions heightened when Chinese nationalists had shelled the U.S. merchant vessel, *The Flying Cloud*. Israel and several small states in Southeast Asia were trying to shrug off the yoke from years of servitude and declare their own independence. In Yugoslavia, Marshall Tito was striving to do just the opposite.

In the United State, the nation-wide coal shortage was hitting everyone hard, especially in the upper Midwest where the new year opened under a bitter cold spell. In Cleveland, a transit strike had, for a short time, threatened to shut down the city.

Current affairs at home and abroad were part of the daily routine in Norris Simpson's history classes. Tucked away as they were in a small rural town in Northwest Ohio, the world's problems seemed a universe away. To the boys and girls sitting in the neat, straight rows of desks before him, Simpson knew life revolved around the basics of farm life—feeding and caring for livestock, cooking and cleaning the house and stoking the fires that warmed and sustained them.

But Simpson also wanted to instill in his students a knowledge and understanding of the big world around them. They may be but a small part of the whole, but even the mightiest machine relied on tiny nuts and bolts to function properly.

It was the same approach Simpson had brought to the school's basketball team. With each player a vital cog in the system, Simpson had built the Wildcats into a formidable machine that had rattled off nine straight wins. Usually undersized and often underestimated, Miller City instead relied on quickness, tenacious defense, deadly accuracy from the wings and the baseline and a seemingly unquenchable desire to succeed.

Simpson marveled at the whole situation. How many coaches, fresh out of college and with no prior head coaching experience, could take over a program and run off nine straight wins right off the bat? The odds had to be staggering.

Early on, in those dark and quiet moments before he would drift off to sleep, Simpson had mulled the question over and over in his mind. Then one night it came to him.

What Simpson had found was a group of players who embraced the game as he did. He remembered his days growing up in Findlay, shooting basket after basket as he blinked the spring rains from his eyes or basted under a scorching summer sun as he strove to make one more shot, perfect one more move, jump that little bit higher until fatigue or fading light or gnawing hunger finally drove him from the court.

He saw that same tenacity in the young men he welcomed every day to practice. For them, the game of basketball was a celebration of who they were. It was winning a blue ribbon at the county fair, getting a date with the prettiest girl in school and earning the acceptance and adulation of their peers all rolled into one. And their stage was a hardwood floor with backboards on either end.

Simpson had always had confidence in his coaching ability. Now he had the canvas on which to create. He knew then how hard he could push the boys, how they would respond, how quickly they would adapt, how courageously they would accept his teachings and how ardently they would apply that knowledge to the craft of basketball.

There would be tests, of course. And with the dawn of the new year came a major challenge from the boys from Hamler.

The game with Hamler, another small town just across the border in Henry County, was not a league game for Simpson and his Wildcats. But there was a natural rivalry between the neighboring school districts, and a growing sense of anticipation that was only heightened by Miller City's unbeaten record.

Hamler set out to prove a point quickly, bolting to a 12–8 lead in the first eight minutes of the game. But Simpson's patience and his faith in his system were rewarded. Turning the tide behind its defensive pressure and getting excellent play from Frank and Junior out front, Miller City used a 16–7 edge in the second quarter to go up 24–17 at the half, then put the clamps on to protect a 48–38 victory.

A physical Hamler team took a toll on Miller City's small team. But Simpson relished the win. It was the type of game his team needed heading into the second half of the regular season, a lesson in diligence as well as determination.

Three nights later, on a January 6 night when fans braved icy roads and freezing rain to pack "The Barn," Joe Lammers broke loose for 16 points and Miller City built a dominating 40–12 lead through three quarters in a 54–34 PCL win over Columbus Grove.

A week later, after a rare Tuesday night off, Miller City pushed its unblemished record to 12–0 and moved into a tie for first place in the PCL standings by wearing down Pandora 66–37. The "Three

Musketeers" were again at their collective best, with Frank scoring 19 points, Joe 16 and Skip 15.

On January 17, Fort Jennings became the unlucky 13th victim of the Wildcats. Joe again scored 16 points, Skip tossed in 15 for the second straight game and Dick Barlage added 13 as Miller City bolted to a 14–4 first quarter lead and never looked back.

Looking ahead, though, might prove dangerous. Because looming on the horizon for the Wildcats was Leipsic, the team that knocked them from the tournament the previous season, the team they currently shared first place with in the PCL standings, the team that year in and year out had been an obstacle the Wildcats had too often tripped over.

It would be Miller City's greatest test of the regular season. And Simpson hoped that, in the blast furnace atmosphere of Leipsic's gym, before 1,800 delirious fans, a champion would be forged.

Years later, when men with fading memories or fortified spirits—or both—discussed the Miller City-Leipsic game of 1950, they more often than not focused upon the what-ifs rather than the what-fors.

What if Bud Snyder, one of Leipsic's best players, had not been injured in a New Year's Eve accident and missed the game?

What if Bob Weaver, another regular, hadn't gotten into early foul trouble?

What if Paul Fenstermaker likewise hadn't joined Weaver on the bench, also a victim of personal fouls, in the second half?

The what-for was that the game of the season turned out not to be much of a game at all.

Before a packed house of nearly 2,000 fans in Leipsic's gymnasium, the expected barn-burner between the Putnam County League leaders never heated up.

For their part, the Wildcats stoked the fire, scoring the first five points of the game and scorching the nets for a 17–9 first-quarter lead. Leipsic did fan the flames with a second-quarter rally, cutting the deficit to 24–20 at the half, then pulling within a basket when Don Ruben opened the third quarter with a jumper.

But when things got tight, Simpson slapped on that tenacious press of his, and the Wildcats stepped it up a notch. Dick Barlage started dominating inside, and Skip and Joe nailed a couple of jumpers from the wings. When Leipsic extended its defense to pressure the outside shots, it opened seams in the zone that Frank and Junior slashed through for driving lay-ups.

After Ruben's second-half opening basket, Miller City went on a 15–5 run to open a 39–27 lead heading into the final period. Some sharp shooting from the foul line down the stretch was all the Wildcats then needed to wrap up a 54–34 victory.

Barlage finished with a game-high 18 points. Miller City's depth and balance was the difference, though, with Joe adding 12 points and Skip and Frank 10 each. Ruben led the Vikings with 15.

When the final horn sounded, Simpson shot an approving glance at the scoreboard. In the weeks leading up to the PCL showdown, his Wildcats had played excellent basketball. They were beating teams, though, that they were expected to beat. Now they had knocked off a team whose record and talent was considered as good as theirs, and they had done it convincingly in a hostile, tournament-like atmosphere.

They had walked into the lion's den and come out not only unscathed, but stronger than when they went in.

With three weeks left in the regular season, the Wildcats stood unbeaten and alone atop the league standings. The target on their collective backs, Simpson knew, would only get larger and more distinct. But Simpson also knew that, by their tenacious style of play and their indomitable desire to win, the Wildcats had won over the pre-season critics and stamped themselves worthy of wearing the PCL crown.

In every basketball season, there comes a defining moment that separates the true contenders from the aspiring challengers. It is a moment when it is not the margin of victory that becomes a foundation for greatness, but the magnitude of it.

Basking in the afterglow of Miller City's decisive win, Norris Simpson realized that a pivotal cornerstone had just been set in concrete. And he wondered, and not for the first time, just what kind of a legacy this rag-tag bunch of farm boys with their faded uniforms and their thinning sneakers was beginning to build.

Time would tell.

Four days after beating Leipsic, Miller City won its 15th straight game by disposing of Liberty 52–28 in a non-league match-up. Frank and Skip led the way with 17 points each, and the Wildcats cashed in at the foul line by making 16 of 20 free throws.

Top to bottom, the Wildcats were a good-shooting team. All of the starters and most of the subs could really stroke the ball, a tribute to long hours shooting baskets on the playgrounds and in the haymows.

Natural shooting ability alone was a plus for the team. But making free throws was a passion of Simpson's.

"You ought to make 100 percent of them because nobody's guarding you," he'd yell at least once during practice.

That was typical of Simpson's approach. A disciplinarian and a taskmaster, he never missed an opportunity to stress the basic fundamentals—positioning on offense, positioning on defense, positioning for rebounds, squaring up to the basket, passing, footwork, ball handling.

From the moment he opened his first practice, Simpson knew he didn't have the personnel to match up man-for-man with some of the teams on his schedule. So he looked for ways to even the playing field.

He saw in his players the desire and tenacity to win. If he could also instill in them the discipline of his offensive and defensive schemes, the combination would be unbeatable.

So far that had been the case. That is why he prodded and chided his players at practice after practice about the smallest details, even something as seemingly insignificant as a foul shot.

Besides, there was strategy involved. At the time, teams had the option of either shooting two free throws or taking the ball out of bounds if the first foul shot was made. It proved to be a decisive factor in many games as the Wildcats made free throws and kept possession of the ball as the final minutes slipped away.

That is why, on the day after the Liberty win, Simpson was concerned as practice drew to a close. One of the final things the team did every day was shoot free throws. Usually there was pending punishment—running laps—for a poor performance.

One player Simpson never had to worry about was Skip Meyer. A pure shooter, he could drain foul shots with his eyes closed. But Skip seemed a tad off today. He'd seemed a step slow in practice, too, and a might pale.

One thing Miller City could not afford was to have one of its best players get sick at this point in the season. So far, Simpson considered himself very lucky. Only one starter had missed a single game and that was because the funeral for John Lammers, Joe Lammers' older brother and a huge fan of the Wildcats, was the same day as the matchup with Ottawa Public.

Skip sucked it up, though, and finished strong. But on the ride home, Joe also noticed something different in his friend's demeanor.

"You feeling alright, Skip? You look a bit peaked."

"I think I overdid it today." Skip answered, a sly grin on his face. "But, man, was it worth it."

"What'd you do?"

"Well, you know how warm it was today. It must have been near 60 when I came to school this morning. It felt so much like spring that, before class, I snuck off down to Shorty's and got me a couple of ice cream bars."

Shorty's was a little family-owned store in Miller City and a favorite hangout for the kids. It wasn't a bad place. But Simpson, a stickler for his players' conduct off the court as well as on, wasn't fond of his players hanging out at the joint.

"Coach wouldn't like you hanging out at Shorty's," Joe said. "But a couple of ice cream bars shouldn't affect you none."

"Well, it was more than a couple," Skip went on. "I went back when we had our morning break, went back again at lunch time and stopped again after school."

"Well, how many did you eat?" Joe persisted.

"Twelve," Skip said. "And they was all good. I was feeling it that last hour of practice, though. And I was afraid if Coach found out, we'd still be in there running laps and shooting foul shots."

The way things were going for Miller City, a heat wave seemed suitably appropriate.

On a balmy night in late January, the Wildcats had journeyed to Liberty Township, made 16 of 20 foul shots, and planted a 52–28 whooping on the home team.

A few nights later, still basking in spring-like weather and the communal warmth a winning basketball program can generate, the Wildcats torched Blanchard 81–37.

Both games were carbon copy, textbook examples of the style of play the Wildcats had come to master under Simpson's leadership—close first quarters as the Wildcats poked and probed for any weakness in the opponent; a faster pace in the second period as Miller City began to orchestrate and then execute its game plan; a dominating third quarter when that stifling press took the spunk right out of the opposition; and then milking out another win with machine-like efficiency.

It was a system that worked time and again as the Wildcats

stacked one victory on top of another. Liberty was Miller City's 15th straight victim. Blanchard went down, and the winning streak reached 16.

More and more people who had never heard of the town were checking their road maps for the tiny flyspeck of a town named Miller City.

Home games were always sold out. But even Ferd Ball had noticed the unfamiliar faces of the clever and the curious who somehow managed to squeeze into "The Barn" to stand deep in the corners and hopefully get a glimpse of this group of Mighty Mites. Most left shaking their heads, as unimpressed by the physical stature of the team as they were amazed by its execution and precision.

Miller City residents who worked in bigger towns like Ottawa or Defiance or Findlay or Lima enjoyed an enhanced status among their co-workers, and it was rare when a coffee break or a lunch hour didn't involve a discussion about Norris Simpson and his unbeaten Wildcats.

Businesses in town, like John Konst's Barber Shop, benefited as well. Still trimming hair at 83, old John never missed a chance to tell a customer that, no sir-ee, in all his years, he'd never seen anything like it. Oh, Miller City had had some good teams over the years. But this team, this here team had that something special that separates good from great.

The entire school system would also benefit from the Wildcats' outstanding success. A few years earlier, voters in the district had accepted a bond issue to build a new school. With those plans still in the works, an additional $50,000 was requested and agreed upon to include a new gymnasium as well.

Through no intentions of his own, Simpson had been accorded almost heroic status in the community, cast as the tall, dark stranger who had ridden into town on a white steed and turned hardwood despair into prosperity.

But he squirmed under the spotlight.

His arenas were the classroom and the basketball court. And in those venues, he was master of his domain, assertive, confident, totally in control. Out in public, he was cordial and polite and customarily accepted the plaudits piled upon him by a grateful following. But he never envisioned himself as a savior, nor pretended to be one. He was a coach and a teacher simply doing what coaches and teachers are trained to do.

That is why he approached every day, every practice, every game with the kind of contagious intensity that had become a trademark of his basketball team.

And that is why, with the regular season winding down, Simpson continued to instill in his players the idea that, despite their string of 16 straight wins, their best games and their biggest victories were not in their past, but in their future.

It seemed ironic in a way that, with the Putnam County League title on the line for Miller City, the Wildcats would be facing Glandorf for the championship trophy.

On one hand, you had Norris Simpson, the striking, first-year coach right out of college who had molded a scrappy group of players into an unbeaten juggernaut.

On the opposing bench sat Joe Nienberg, who had been coaching that same group of players the past few years before leaving for a similar position at Glandorf.

Miller City had won an earlier match-up between the two schools, 63–26. A Glandorf victory now would have made the season for the Dragons, but it was not to be.

With Joe Lammers having one of his best games of the season—21 points—and Frank and Skip combining for 34 more, Miller City's "Three Musketeers" played the last home game of their careers like men possessed. Glandorf kept it close early on.

But Miller City used a 17–6 run to go ahead 32–15 at the half. When it was over, the Wildcats had nearly doubled the Dragons, 78–40.

Now 17–0 overall, Miller City also improved to 11–0 in the PCL and assured itself of no less than a tie for the league championship. But one obstacle remained between the Wildcats and an undefeated regular season and outright PCL title. That obstacle was Ottawa Sts. Peter and Paul.

Eventually, Ottawa's public and parochial schools would join Glandorf and consolidate. And eventually, Ottawa-Glandorf would become a basketball dynasty, mold its own strong tradition and win a state championship of its own.

In 1950, however, the schools were still separate. And, as is often the case when schools are close and bunched together, there was the issue of protecting one's turf from neighboring schools and outsiders alike.

You could sense an almost territorial possessiveness at times. It was not so evident within the city limits, where players from Sts. Peter and Paul and those from Ottawa Public may have grown up on the same street in houses side by side. But for outsiders, the underlying intensity was a tangible thing.

There wasn't a man on the Miller City roster who at one time or another hadn't felt like a foreigner in a strange land within the Ottawa city limits. Oh, there might be the nodding acknowledgment when they went into town to get a new suit at Gustwiller's or school supplies at Frey's or when they took a date to see a movie at the Rex Theater downtown.

But it was always understood that this was their turf, and everyone else was only visiting.

So it was that, when Miller City stepped into the SPPS gym for the final game of the 1949–50 regular season, the Wildcats were viewed as an invading conqueror from the north, swooping in to carry away the PCL championship trophy as the spoils of victory.

The Saints, mired in the middle of the PCL pack, had nothing at all to lose. But they could salvage much from the dying season, pride if nothing else, if they could turn back the invading horde and protect what was theirs—their turf.

If this upstart bunch from Miller City wanted an outright PCL championship, SPPS was determined to make them earn every bit of it. Stubbornly, Sts. Peter and Paul put up a fight. Things got rough. Things got physical. It was body-on-body from one end of the floor to the other as the home team staked a claim to what was theirs.

The Saints led 10–5 after one quarter of play and were still on top 14–13 late in the first half.

They were winning the small battles man-to-man. And by doing so they hoped they could also win the war.

But the outsiders had something to prove as well. Well aware that many considered them rubes, hicks and bumpkins who spent the majority of their days shoveling manure and slopping hogs, they now had a common battle field—a basketball court—on which to challenge and change those perceptions.

This was their big chance to win the one thing that they felt they'd never gotten on those many, many trips to the big city. This was their chance to win their respect.

Perhaps that was the desperation that ignited the rally as Miller City scored the last 4 points of the second quarter to take a 17–14 lead and a huge measure of confidence into the locker room at the half.

It was in the quiet closeness of the locker room where Simpson did his best work. On the sidelines, he could be many things—a drill sergeant, a cheerleader, a traffic cop—and all at the same time. But in the locker room, a sanctuary for just him and his players, he could be more of a mentor, a confident, a friend.

He was not much older than these scrap-iron players, and not so long removed from the hardwood that he no longer felt the same competitive fires that fueled their passion for the game. Perhaps that is why his players had come to accept his leadership unflinchingly. Simpson's thoroughness and attention to detail served him well as he broke down, player by player, what could be exploited, adjusted and used to their advantage.

Not once did the Wildcats leave the locker room without a concrete plan and a sense of purpose. It would pay off once again this night, as Miller City gradually took control of the game in the third quarter, expanding the lead point by point until it reached 32–25 by the end of the period.

During the break, Simpson reiterated one last time the importance of melding fundamentals and execution with desire and determination. It was a recipe that had worked all season and would work once again. With Skip, Joe and Frank leading the assault, Miller City capped its unbeaten season with a dazzling display of basketball, outscoring the Saints 19–10 to put the icing on a 51–35 victory.

Joe finished with 15 points, Skip 13 and Frank 10. Roy Meyer, the flashy sophomore who was becoming a dynamic, late-season spark for the team, had 9 points in another solid game off the bench.

When it was all over, Simpson felt an overwhelming sense of relief. His players had not only shocked the experts by winning the league championship, they had achieved something only one other team in PCL history (Ottoville, 1935) had done. They had gone through the regular season undefeated.

It was a phenomenal achievement and one Simpson took great personal pride in. But as the fans cheered and the celebration rolled on, Simpson also understood clearly that while one season was over, another season was about to begin.

The spitter splatter of a steady rain on the window ledge woke Norris Simpson from what had been a peaceful sleep, his most restful night it seemed in months.

Usually up and about early, Simpson instead sank back beneath the covers and allowed himself a few stolen moments of reflective bliss.

Had it been less than 12 hours ago that his Miller City team of rag-tag farm boys had beaten Ottawa Sts. Peter and Paul to not only win the Putnam County League championship, but also to polish off an unbeaten regular season in the process?

Could anyone, especially the fanatic faithful from Miller City, have imagined such a season?

Not Simpson. At least not the Norris Simpson who, three months out of college, had accepted the position as head coach of the tiny school in the rustic outback of Northwest Ohio.

Never in his days at Findlay College, when he had already

decided to pursue a career in teaching and coaching, had he imagined anything like this—a community so small, its entire population was about what he'd seen every Sunday morning at church back in Findlay; a school so small that, if they packed in well, you could squeeze an entire graduating class in one good-sized car; a gymnasium so small, you could almost grab a rebound off one backboard, turn, step and lay it in off the other without being called for traveling; a team so small that, had they walked into a Class A school, they could easily be mistaken for a junior high team; one good basketball to practice with; and uniforms so faded and worn that, early on, Simpson pitched one set and sent his players out the rest of the season in the one remaining pair.

Oh, Simpson had seen flashes of talent early on. But it was at times undisciplined and often in need of a refresher course in fundamentals.

But it was also the perfect crucible for an idealistic young coach. Where an older, more established man might have balked at the situation, Simpson saw it as a proving ground for the fresh ideas and textbook theories that had been a part of his recent studies.

Determined to make the best of the occasion, Simpson came up with a plan, then got to work.

First, he drilled his team mercilessly. By getting his players in the best shape of their lives, he hoped to compensate for their physical limitations with stamina and hustle.

He learned quickly that all of his players could handle the ball, and most could shoot the lights out if left unguarded. But he also worked them tirelessly on the drudgery of defense and rebounding for those times when the shots would not fall.

Week by week and game by game, he stuck to his plan. And gradually, something miraculous happened. One win became two, and two became four. And as the wins piled up, Simpson noticed the team becoming a living extension of his own goals and ideals.

The more he drilled them, the more they responded. The more

he barked, the more bite they put into their game. The more he demanded of them, the more they demanded of themselves.

Winning was never, ever a sure thing. But as Simpson quickly learned, losing soon became something unacceptable to this band of undersized, over-achieving Mighty Mites.

Nestled beneath the covers, Simpson could have allowed himself to become enveloped in the smugness of success. But that was neither his nature nor his style. He'd already made plans to take this day off to return home to Findlay to visit his parents, maybe look up his old coach, Carl Bachman, and catch his alma mater in action. The Findlay High Trojans were having a banner season of their own, but his own schedule had allowed little time to see them play.

Besides, soon enough it would be back to work. The county tournament, the first level of post-season play, was set to get underway Tuesday and Simpson, ever the perfectionist, wanted to be prepared.

Simpson liked the fact that the county tournament started so soon after the regular season. Less time for relapse and distraction that way.

But he was concerned as well. As a player, he'd seen firsthand the hopes and dreams of talented teams go up in smoke because of a few silly mistakes or one off night. There was a cutting edge to tournament play. It was one-and-done, like a giant pickup game involving the entire state, where teams traveled from town to town and court to court.

Win, and you live to play again. Lose, and you take your basketball and go home.

Simpson knew the county tournament would be a daunting gauntlet. Every team in the field was a vanquished victim who would be given the opportunity to knock off the unbeaten Wildcats and exact a measure of revenge.

The PCL's pre-season favorites—Ottoville, Leipsic, Continental—would all be laying in wait.

Miller City had denied them all a league championship trophy.

But Simpson knew well that a tournament win over the Wildcats would go a long way towards salving those wounds.

Those battles, if they did materialize, were still a ways off, though. Today, Simpson had other plans. As he threw back the covers and began to get ready, Simpson cast a quick glance out the window. The rain, he noticed, had let up a bit. But the skies remained cloudy and threatening.

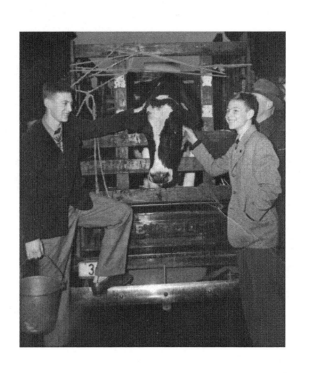

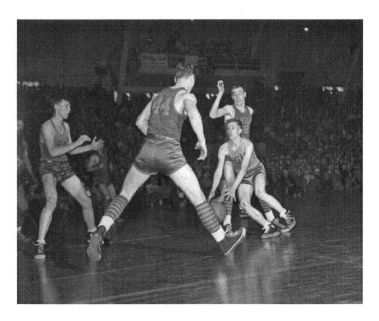

Minnie Beckman and Mary Noon, both widowed, were two of the most respected ladies in Miller City and perhaps the Wildcats' staunchest fans.

Rarely did Minnie and Mary miss a game. Side by side they always sat, familiar figures game after game. There were no reserved seats in "The Barn." But there was an inherent, unwritten policy that the same two seats, like pews in the local church, would be always be saved for Minnie and Mary.

Dignified as they were, they would let out an occasional whoop and a holler when things were going especially good, or wring their hands and grab the other's arm when they were not.

And after every game, as the people filed out the doors, some-one would invariably ask them, "See ya next game ladies?" And one or the other would invariably reply, "God willing and the creeks don't rise."

As the 1949–50 regular season came to an end and teams prepared for the upcoming Putnam County basketball tournament, their jestful refrain may have been a premonition.

That winter had been an odd one, even by the recollections of the grizzled old-timers who had seen a half century of northwest Ohio winters and more. Bitterly cold at times, the winter of '49–50 had its share of blustery blizzards. But each Arctic blast had been followed by unseasonable warmth. And rain. Lots and lots of rain.

By the middle of February Ray Burkholder, newly installed as the county's National Weather Observer, reported that the area had already been doused by nearly double that month's average of 1.6 inches of rain. Then came the weekend of February 12.

A cold front greeted early risers and church-goers that Sunday morning. But on its heels was another balmy blast working its way up through the Midwest from the Gulf of Mexico.

By Sunday night, it had begun to snow huge flakes that piled up like an endless white canvas upon the ground. By Monday morning, when coaches and administrators from every school in the county sloshed their way to the county courthouse in Ottawa for the tournament drawing, there was three inches covering the roadways and fields.

Some would consider it odd that a basketball drawing would be held in the county courthouse instead of a centrally located school or gymnasium. But in Putnam County, where basketball has always been held in high esteem, to gather in a room just down the hall from where death and taxes and judgments are handed down seemed a logically appropriate location.

Norris Simpson, a novice at this thing called a tournament draw, shifted nervously. As the other coaches filed in, they gamely shook his hand, patted him on the back and remarked what a great job he and his team had done in winning the league championship. But he couldn't help feeling like he was the new kid on the block and everyone else wanted his toys.

All 13 schools in the county would take part in the tournament. Four teams were seeded, with Miller City the obvious N0.1 pick.

The other three seeds went to Leipsic, which edged Ottoville to finish second in the league standings, Ottoville and Continental. Because there were at least 12 teams in the county tournament, three would advance to the district.

Though a rookie at county tournaments and seeding meetings, Simpson kept his wits about him. Using the N0.1 seed, he positioned Miller City in a bracket with three teams—Fort Jennings, Vaughnsville and Blanchard—that his Wildcats had handled easily. Miller City had gone through the regular season unbeaten, but he astutely rationalized that the tournament was a brand new start and it would be better for his Wildcats to get their feet wet than to dive headlong into the shark-infested competition.

Early Putnam County tournaments had been held at the armory in Ottawa. It suited the needs at the time, but the armory had limited seating, was small compared to some of the more expansive gymnasiums built later on and posed problems to players because of an overhanging balcony. Scheduling for the county tournament was also an adventure. Games were usually played back-to-back from morning 'til night, with teams often playing two, sometimes three times a day.

When Leipsic built its new gymnasium, a massive structure capable of seating 1,800, the county tournament was moved there. Good thing, too, because had the tournament remained at the armory in Ottawa, it never would have been completed on time in 1950.

As Simpson and the other county coaches left the courthouse, they were greeted by rumbling thunder and a drenching deluge. A warm front had sped in on the heels of Sunday's cold wave. The three inches of snow that had fallen overnight quickly melted and mixed with the downpour that, before the day was out, would drop another three inches of rain.

With the ground already saturated, water poured off the fields and filled to the brim every ditch and stream in the area. The mighty Blanchard River, which snaked in from the east and hugged the south edge of Ottawa, quickly filled as well, then spewed over its banks and began creeping, higher and higher, down every street in town.

Eventually, the waters crested and began to recede, but not before Ottawa had suffered its worst flood in 37 years. Every community in the county had seen its share of high water as well. But Leipsic's school and the gymnasium were 10 miles north of the Blanchard, and the damage was not as severe.

For many, there would be detours around low spots and flooded roads. But the 1950 county tournament, delayed a few days by the flood, would still go on. And that was good news indeed for a nondescript Miller City team about to embark on one of the most amazing runs in Ohio basketball history.

Norris Simpson stared out of his apartment window and caught himself mumbling the lines from a poem he'd had to read in one of his English classes years before, something about, "Water, water everywhere…"

But he could not remember the rest. His mind was totally occupied with thoughts of his team and the rain-delayed county tournament. In a way, he resented Mother Nature and her untimely flood. Some coaches might have welcomed the break after a grueling season in which the pressure mounted game by game and win by win. It would have been an opportune time to rest weary bodies and rejuvenate spent spirits.

But Simpson didn't coach that way. He firmly believed that when you hone a tool to a razor's edge you don't just let it hang in the shed. You use it. And he had honed his team to perfection.

As the season wore on, he had tried to keep his practices from becoming a mundane repetition of fundamental drills and a rehash of opponents' tendencies. What his team needed now was competition, but the flood waters lapping at his doorstep were making that impossible.

Frustrated, Simpson paced the floors of his apartment. In his mind, he pictured each of his starters, their backups and the matchups each would face in the tournament. And gradually his frustration subsided, replaced by a calming acceptance.

Basketball, he knew, was a passion for his players, a saucy mistress who lured them away from chores and errands and everyday obligations of necessity. She was a siren calling them to run and play hide-and-seek from the toil that marked their daily lives.

But the land, now that was their livelihood. It put food on their tables and strength in their spirits. It was the one concrete foundation supporting most of the family structures in the area, and it was an unshakable foundation.

Simpson had seen that firsthand on those days when, just starting out, he had made his rounds of the farms to meet prospective players and their families and ended up lugging bales of hay or buckets of slop right along with them.

Simpson understood that the flood waters lapping at his door step were lapping at theirs, too. And if things got worse, more than a practice or two would be washed away.

Miller City was scheduled to open the Putnam County tournament against Fort Jennings on Tuesday, February 14. Because of the flood, the Wildcats didn't hit the floor until that Friday, three days later.

In a hastily called practice the day before the tournament and again in the pre-game locker room, Simpson stressed the importance of getting a quick lead and setting a good pace early in the game. He knew that some teams would see Miller City's unbeaten record and be intimidated, and he did not want to lose whatever edge—psychological or otherwise—he could gain.

The last thing Simpson wanted was some club that finished in the lower division of the league standings thinking that because the regular season was over Miller City had regressed into just another run-of-the-mill team.

But if Simpson had any doubts that the delay would adversely affect his team, his fears were quickly put to rest. Skip, shouldering the role of team leader, made sure of that.

There was a bit of rust on the Wildcats. Three days of slogging through flood waters would do that. But Skip took control early, slashing inside for driving lay-ups and teaming with Dick Barlage to establish a dominance underneath. Miller City broke out to a 12–5 lead after the first quarter, struggled through a mechanical 7–7 deadlock in the second period, then reestablished its control in the third quarter by going back to its strength—the press—to widen the gap. The Wildcats nearly tripled Fort Jennings in the third quarter, outscoring the Musketeers 14–5 to go up 33–17. Subs and reserves finished off the 48–28 victory.

Skip led the Wildcats with 17 points. Barlage added 10 as Miller City, constantly attacking the basket, got over half of its points from its "big men."

Frank had his usual strong floor game out front and scored 9 points. His little brother, Roy, who was becoming a stronger and stronger threat off the bench, had 7.

Miller City had beaten Fort Jennings by almost 30 points (58–29) during the regular season. But Simpson could abide the 20-point margin in the tournament opener.

His team, he knew, wasn't the only one that had progressed throughout the year. But each game would offer new demands and new challenges, and there was little time to prepare. Saturday was filled with a full slate of lower bracket, first-round games, Sunday was a day off and the Wildcats were scheduled to face Blanchard, which had edged Vaughnsville 47–44 in its opener, on Monday.

Miller City had blitzed Blanchard 81–37 during the regular season. But as any knowledgeable basketball fan—and Putnam County was crawling with them—knew, it was never as easy the second time around, and tournament time always seemed to bring out the best in teams.

Most of the first-round tournament games matched one of the top teams in the league against one of the worst. Still, it was not too surprising that all of those first-round games except one were decided by 10 points or less. That is the nature of tournament play, when underdogs with nothing but pride to play for become bulldogs backed into a corner by the finality of the situation. And favorites with high expectations become nervous and skittish under the pressure.

Simpson, always a student of the game, digested it all as Monday's game approached. A taskmaster who always expected the utmost from his team, he had decided to set a certain tone right from the opening tip of this seemingly predestined second-round game.

Miller City fans, then, were not surprised to see their head coach up off the bench, barking orders and defensive assignments from one end of the floor to the other. Nor were they stunned when, after one errant pass sailed out of bounds, his clipboard made a resounding *whack* on the bench beside him and split cleanly in two. It was not the first time that had happened, nor would it be the last. A surprising sum of Simpson's first-year pay, it seemed, would go to replacement clipboards.

Simpson's intensity had the desired effect, however, and Blanchard's slim upset hopes took the brunt of it.

Miller City blasted out of the gates, built a 15–1 lead in the first 6 minutes of play, and never slowed down. The final score—61–32—wasn't as one-sided as the earlier match-up. But a message, as subtle as a bee sting, had been sent just the same.

Skip didn't have to carry as much of the load this time. He had 11 points. Frank led the team with 14, Junior McDonald also scored 11, and Joe Lammers, surprisingly scoreless in the tournament opener, had 10. All of that balanced scoring came in the first three quarters before Simpson once again turned the final period over to his reserves.

Clare Gratz, a second-team all-PCL selection, scored 15 points for Blanchard, but Miller City's stifling defense limited the rest of the team to just 17.

Miller City wasn't the only team in the tournament hitting its stride, however. Leipsic, Ottoville and Continental also won second-round games, and all three did so convincingly. As most of the experts had expected, the area's top four teams had all advanced to the county tournament semifinals.

The terms *rematch* and *revenge* were now being bantered back and forth over morning coffee and after-work beers. And since only three of the four remaining teams would advance to the district tournament, a sense of urgency was brewing as well.

Spirits—in school and around town—were obviously running high after Miller City's winning streak hit 20 games with the tournament wins over Fort Jennings and Blanchard. There was a euphoric air of expectancy in the community.

But Simpson kept his team focused on the on the job at hand. He saw the tournament as more like a marathon than a series of sprints, and he wanted his players prepared for the long haul.

Officials, hoping to get things back on schedule, had crammed into nine days a tournament expected to last almost two weeks. There was little time to rest tired bodies and less time to prepare for upcoming opponents.

And on the horizon loomed an old nemesis—Leipsic, the same team that had knocked Miller City out of the county tournament a year earlier.

When the two teams met during the regular season, both were unbeaten in league play, and despite Miller City's 13–0 overall slate, the Wildcats were considered an underdog on the Vikings' home floor.

Simpson knew the Vikings were not at full strength. Injuries had hurt the team. But Simpson also knew that a lion is most dangerous when it is wounded. And this lion was on its home turf.

For the second time that season, a packed house was on hand to see the pre-season favorites take on the little upstart team from Miller City. And when the Vikings took the early lead on a free throw, more than a few Vikings' fans felt that victory and vindication were at last at hand.

But Miller City spat on its hands and hunkered down to work. It wasn't so noticeable on the offensive end. Dribbling, passing and shooting came naturally to the Wildcats' players. It was on the defensive end where the dirty work needed to get done.

Hounding Leipsic from one end of the floor to the other—trapping, pressing, scrapping—Miller City denied every pass and contested every shot. The Vikings did convert a couple of free throws, but they wouldn't connect on their first basket until Paul Fenstermaker, who would lead Leipsic with 12 points that night, finally fired one in midway through the second quarter. By then Miller City had expanded on a 14–4 first quarter advantage and was rolling up a 24–13 lead by the break.

Leipsic showed its mettle by staging a third-quarter comeback that cut the deficit to 6 points (34–28) late in the third quarter. But Miller City looked to high-percentage inside shots, with Junior driving the lane and dishing off to Skip or Dick for easy lay-ins.

Miller City's lead crept back to 8 points, then 10, then 12. With Skip (17) and Dick (16) combining for 33 points and the five starters never leaving the floor, Miller City ran away with a 50–35 win and claimed one of the two spots in the county tournament final.

Just two nights later, Miller City went after its second championship in two weeks. The Wildcats already had the Putnam County League regular season title in hand. Winning in the county tournament would add some more hardware to the growing collection in the trophy case and reaffirm the team's claim as the best in the area.

Everyone expected Ottoville, one of the pre-season PCL favorites, to be the Wildcats' opponent in the final. But the Big Green, perhaps looking a bit too far ahead, were upended by Continental in the other PCL tournament semifinal as 18-point efforts by Dick Kirkendall and Dick Sanders led the Pirates to a stunningly one-sided 59–42 victory.

Simpson and his players had been expecting a rematch with Ottoville as well. Now they had to switch gears, mentally more than physically, and expect the unexpected.

This game, too, would be a rematch. The two teams had met twice during the regular season, including a 37–34 thriller in the 1949–50 opener that, as much as anything, planted the seeds of success for the rest of the season. It was a win, but more than that, Simpson often referred to that game as the perfect schematic for what his team needed to do to improve.

It was the adjustments made after that opening game that allowed Miller City to take the PCL rematch between the two schools rather easily, 42–22. Now Simpson worried that the schematic could work in reverse, that Continental might use those earlier games to develop the type of game plan that just might turn the tables.

Continental would be dangerous. That became apparent when the Pirates jumped on top of Miller City right out of the gates.

This team had obviously prepared itself well for the rematch.

Miller City seemed nervous at first. Playing a team the third time in one season can obviously sow seeds of doubt. For weeks, though, Simpson had been drilling his team on the importance of defense, especially in tournament play. No matter how smoothly an offense runs, shots don't always fall. But defense is always constant, a foundation built with hustle and determination that can hold a team firm until the offense begins to click.

Throughout the tournament, opponents would marvel at the tenacity of the Miller City defense. Man-to-man, zone, press—it didn't matter. Teams rarely got an uncontested shot or a clear look at the basket.

Pressure was the key. Miller City applied it. Opponents cracked under it.

It took a toll again in the county tournament championship game. Continental scored two baskets in the first two minutes, but made just five more in the next two-and-a-half quarters. Miller

City's pressure forced mistakes, the mistakes became opportunities and the Wildcats' smooth transition game—from defense to offense in the blink of an eye—capitalized.

Miller City took the lead at 6–4 and quickly hit its stride. The Wildcats led 12–5 after the first quarter and 20–8 at the half. A 13–6 run in the third quarter gave Simpson and his crew all the cushion they needed to weather a Continental comeback bid that was too little too late to make much difference in the 43–32 final score.

Frank played a masterful game for Miller City. Named earlier in the week to the all-PCL first team Frank was the perfect floor leader for the Wildcats, triggering the offense, igniting the defense, making the kind of decisions expected of a team leader. He also finished with a team-high 13 points. Skip added 10 points and Dick and Joe 7 each to a balanced attack.

Since the top three teams in the county tournament advanced to the district, there was not a cut-throat, do-or-die atmosphere surrounding the county tournament final. That kind of drama was reserved for the consolation game, however, where Ottoville avenged its regular season loss to Leipsic and beat the Vikings in a nail-biter, 38–34.

When it was over, when only the custodian and a few tournament officials remained in the Leipsic gymnasium, Simpson cradled the county tournament trophy and breathed a heavy sigh of relief.

It had been a frantic and hectic two weeks. But his team had weathered the storm—on the court and off—to come through it unscathed. Now they were in the district, and things would get tougher day by day and game by game.

Simpson knew bigger challenges lay ahead. But as he slung his overcoat over his shoulder and headed for the door, he thought for about the thousandth time that there just might be something special about this team, something special indeed.

Norris Simpson felt twitchy.

He squirmed. He fidgeted. He rocked side to side, first on one foot, then on the other.

This was new stuff to him.

A reporter from one of the area papers had come down to interview Simpson for an article about the upcoming district tournament.

Totally in command at practice and during a game, unfazed by towering opponents or intimidating coaches, Simpson suddenly found himself a bit unnerved by a smallish man with spectacles and a pad and a pencil in his hands.

Simpson hadn't dealt with reporters during the season. Come game night, Leo Lammers kept the official scorebook and Bill Bellman and Paul Hermiller kept the team's stats. A day after the game, sometimes two, one of those men or team manager Charlie Warnimont would call the results in to the local paper, the Putnam County Sentinel. When the weekly paper hit the streets, you could get all the pertinent information you needed—quarter-by-quarter totals, leading scorers, league and overall records.

But this was new ground. This wasn't idle chit-chat over a cup of coffee at the corner restaurant, a card game at the VFW or a few beers at the local watering hole. What was said here would appear in indelible ink the next day. There was historic finality in that cold, hard fact and Simpson, a history teacher, wondered if years from now someone might read his words in the archives and consider them insightful or prophetic or merely the ramblings of a young rookie coach.

The reporter was persistent; Simpson a bit guarded.

"You're 22–0," the reporter said. "You must have quite a talented team."

"Nothing special," Simpson answered. "They're just a hard-working bunch of farm boys who love to play the game."

"Who are the stars on your team, coach?"

"We don't have a star player, really," Simpson said. "Frank Schroeder is our floor leader. He scores enough and triggers our defense. But the thing about Frank is that he makes good decisions out on the floor. He doesn't make mistakes.

"Ralph Meyer—he goes by Skip—plays in the middle mostly. He's not big, but he's quick and can hit the baseline shot. He and Frank are our only two all-league players.

"Joe Lammers is at one forward and Dick Barlage at the other. Joe's a good outside shot, and he hits the boards well for his size. Dick's sorta hefty, but he's hard to move when he gets positioned down low, he rebounds well, and he has a soft little hook shot that's hard to stop.

"Those guys are all seniors. Our other starter is a sophomore, Ray McDonald. Everybody calls him Junior. He's a quick, little left-hander who's really good at driving to the basket and dishing it off. He leads us in assists.

"Jerry Kuhlman is one of the first guys off the bench and Skip's younger brother Roy, a sophomore, has really been playing well here late in the season and in tournament. A couple of other boys—Karl Inkrott, Vern Schroeder, Don Alt and Bill Zeigler—give us some pretty good minutes, too."

"Coach, I see by your scores you can really light it up—82 points against Vaughnsville, 81 against Blanchard, 72 against Glandorf, a lot of other scores in the 50s and 60s."

"Yeah, our boys can shoot, no doubt about that. But if we don't play good defense, we might get run right out of the gym."

"What defense do you prefer, Coach? Man-to-man? Zone?"

"I always felt defense was more about hard work and hustle and determination than about any particular style," Simpson replied. "You do what you have to do. We don't have the height to match up with some teams. We're not as deep as others. But we're pretty quick. And one thing we can do against anybody is get after 'em on defense, and that's what we try to do."

"You're 22–0 Coach. You have the best record in the field. But there are 10 other teams in the district, and some of them have some pretty impressive records, too. What do you know about them?"

"Well, we played Ottoville and Continental. They're in our league, and they're both pretty good teams. We played Hamler, too, and they gave us quite a game. I saw where Ridgeville is something like 20–1 and Haviland is 17–1. Archbold's in there, too, and they always seem to have a pretty strong program.

"But to be honest with you, the team I worry about most is us. We can't control what other teams do. We don't decide what offense they run or what defense they throw at us. The only thing we can control is what we do. That has to be our top priority, our top concern."

"It seems to have worked for you so far, Coach. Looks like your Mighty Mites have met every challenge."

"They have, and I'm proud of these guys. I've asked an awful lot of them, but they've always come out and played like champions. That's all any coach can ask of his team."

The waiting was driving Norris Simpson crazy. But he knew there was nothing he could do about it.

Eleven teams had qualified for the Class B district tournament that would be staged over a two-week period at Defiance High School. But because of the way the pairings panned out, one rat-tail match-up and four first-round games would be played and in the books before Simpson's Miller City Wildcats would step onto the floor.

Down time was not necessarily a good thing, not at this point anyway. It was late in a long season, and practices could bog down into drudgery for the teams still alive in the tournament.

The sharp edge of efficiency honed by tough competition could now be dulled by inactivity.

But Simpson was not one to idly accept the inevitable. Ever the tactician, the strategist, the motivator, he used the district sched-ule to his advantage. Playing the last game of the opening round meant he could scout and analyze every other team in the field, charting strengths and weaknesses and team tendencies. And so he became a fixture at the tournament, perched in the same spot high in the bleachers night after night, taped-up clipboard in hand as he charted every team that could be a future opponent.

Simpson understood that some time away from the basketball court might be beneficial for his players as well. The Wildcats were still the talk of the town in the tiny farming community. Local hangouts like Mac & Rita's and Shorty's became favorite gathering spots for the faithful to rehash the recent past and speculate on the future.

But as February melted into March, there were also the pressing needs of everyday life. Livestock still had to be tended to. Spring plowing was not far off, and farm equipment had to be repaired and prepared for the planting season.

With their next game still a week away, players could revert back to a bit of normalcy in their day to day lives. They could make a date, take their sweetheart to a movie in Ottawa, plan an outing with guys who were just friends and not teammates.

Or they could get together and shoot hoops—nothing more, nothing less—or go one-on-one or play a game of H-O-R-S-E. No zone defenses or transition offenses to worry about. Not because there was a district game on the schedule, but because it was something fun to do.

Simpson knew it could be a time to relax and renew. And it might be the last time in a long time they'd have that luxury.

The rout. The rally. The rematch.

In the months immediately following the 1949–50 season, and in the many years spent savoring the memories that immortalized it, Norris Simpson often felt those three little words best summed up not only the 1950 district tournament, but Miller City's miraculous season as well.

The rout, a 66–38 run-away win over Edgerton in the district opener, typified the type of talent on Simpson's team. Undersized in almost every game, the Wildcats still had the shooting touch, the overall quickness and the court savvy to play a very good game of basketball. When it all clicked, it was something beautiful to behold.

The rally, a testament to the competitive fire that burns in the heart of true champions, was a nail-biting 39–38 thriller over a tough Archbold team in round two. The Wildcats led only twice—2–1 after their first basket of the game and 39–38 after the final buzzer.

The rematch was a 38–34 decision over Ottoville in the district championship game. Led by Putnam County League scoring champion Gene Schimmoeller, Ottoville fielded one of the tallest and most talented teams in the conference. And the district final victory not only mirrored a 48–44 win over the Big Green during the regular season, it also instilled in Simpson's young men a sense that no matter who filled the opposing uniforms, with grit and hustle and determination they could hold their own with any team in the state.

Outwardly, Simpson always exuded an air of confidence. But inside he was prone to the same fidgety uncertainty every coach feels before facing a new opponent.

As usual, Simpson's preparation was impeccable. On the Monday before the district tournament, he had taken his team to Findlay, where Carl Bachman, his former high school coach, allowed the Wildcats to stretch their legs on the big floor at Findlay High School.

Simpson had also scouted every district game so far. Unfortunately, the one opponent he could not scout was the one his team was scheduled to play. Other than Edgerton's 15–5 record, Simpson knew little else about the Bulldogs.

So on a bitter cold Saturday night on the first weekend of March, Miller City and Edgerton squared off on the Defiance High School court. Tentatively at first, they poked and prodded and danced and jabbed like two middleweights on the under card of the main event.

Late in the first quarter, Simpson had seen enough. During a quick time out, he delivered a blistering ultimatum.

His exact words were not recorded. But the message was clear; "Crank it up or go home!"

As usual, his message got through.

Miller City finished the first period with a small run, doubled Edgerton 20–10 in the second quarter to go up 34–20 at the half, then nearly doubled the Bulldogs again—18–10—to open a commanding 52–30 lead heading into the final stretch.

Simpson's senior veterans again led the way. Skip finished with 21 points, Joe 14 and Frank 10. Junior McDonald also had an excellent game, scoring 11 points.

Tom Herman had 17 points for Edgerton. But Miller City's stifling defense held the rest of the Bulldogs' team to a total of 21.

Ottoville, paired in the bracket opposite Miller City, had also won its opener handily, beating a 20–1 Ridgeville squad 52–38. But the team that most concerned Simpson was Archbold.

Simpson had been on hand for Archbold's district win over West Unity. And he had been impressed with what he saw. Hard-nosed and well-coached, Archbold reminded Simpson a lot of his own Wildcats. Fundamentally, the Blue Streaks were as sound as any team in the tournament. They were scrappy and aggressive on defense and patient enough on offense to work for the high percentage shot.

Simpson emphasized all those things to his players in the week leading up to the district semifinal. In the end, it may not have mattered, because it all came down to one of the most heads-up plays in prep tournament history.

Outsiders might have looked simply at the records—Miller City 23–0, Archbold 15–6—and predicted a mismatch. But the Blue Streaks proved to be all that Simpson had expected. And more.

Fired up from the get-go, Archbold erased Miller City's early 2–1 edge, outscored the Wildcats 7–2 the rest of the first quarter, and raced to an 11-point lead midway through the second period.

Miller City fought back to within six (21–15) by the half, but had to overcome an 8-point deficit to still trail by that 5-point margin—32–27—heading into the final period.

Defeat may have been staring Miller City in the face. But Simpson saw no quit in the eyes of his players as they huddled during the break before the fourth quarter.

"You have eight minutes to turn this game around," he told them. "Get after them, and make something happen."

Destiny masquerades in many forms. In the final eight minutes of the district semifinals, it wore a cloak called defense.

Turning up the intensity of its press, trapping and double-teaming at every chance, Miller City's defense threw a blanket over Archbold. The Blue Streaks got off just three shots over those final eight minutes, and connected just once.

Archbold was cashing in at the line, however, just enough to maintain an edge. And with the Wildcats making just 5-of-16 fourth-quarter shots it appeared that tiny edge might be enough.

Still, baskets versus free throws was a two-for-one exchange. And with each shot made, the Wildcats crept closer, eventually cutting the gap to a single point—38–37—with under a minute left.

What happened then remains a point of controversy, even after all these many years.

There was a loose ball; several players went for it, and the ball was knocked out of bounds during the scramble.

But which team touched it last?

One official looked at the other. The other simply looked back.

In that split second of indecision, Skip Meyer made perhaps the definitive play of the tournament. Confidently, he stepped out of bounds, looked expectantly at the referee and extended his hands for the ball.

Perhaps the officials intended to award Miller City the ball anyway.

Or perhaps his bold move swung destiny's pendulum just a bit.

In either case, Meyer was handed the ball. He inbounded it, took a return pass, drove the lane and scored. One account says there were 40 seconds left on the clock. Another says there were 20. One claims there were 6.

The exact time frame seems as fuzzy as the play that created the spectacular finish.

The only certainty is that Miller City had survived to play

again, and one night later the Wildcats were back on the Defiance High School floor. The opponent this time was PCL rival Ottoville, which needed a clutch rally of its own to defeat Haviland-Scott 50–43 in the other semifinal.

Miller City had barely held off the Big Green 48–44 back on December 16 during their regular season match-up. The game shaped up as a Titanic battle between the two best teams in the Putnam County League, with the winner getting to take home the district championship.

Simpson fretted that there was so little time to prepare for the rematch. But he realized that this game would not be about preparation. It would be about courage and guts and the kind of sheer determination every individual chooses to embody.

This was no mid-season game where future opponents were inked onto a calendar. It was not like the county tournament where the top three teams qualified for the next round.

There was a finality to this showdown, as stark and as dire as a car wreck.

Long-time Ottoville coach Louis Heckman ran a strong program, perennially one of the best in the Putnam County League.

And this talented group of players had something to prove.

Three of Ottoville's four losses had come against teams regarded as the elite in the PCL—Miller City, Leipsic and Continental. The other had been to Delphos St. John's, the defending Class B state champion and currently ranked N0.1 among the state's 820 small-school teams. The Big Green had already avenged the loss to Leipsic. Beating Miller City would even the score there as well. And the way the tournament was playing out, it looked like a regional rematch with Delphos St. John's was definitely a possibility.

All the pressure, it seemed, was on Miller City and its 24–0 record. But pressure is also what forges the hardest steel, the brightest diamonds and sometimes, the greatest victories.

In an area where high school basketball reigns supreme, the

1950 district championship game between Miller City and Ottoville is still considered one of the classic all-time match-ups.

Skip Meyer, Frank Schroeder and Joe Lammers, Miller City's offensive leaders throughout the season, looked to carry the team. But Ottoville's aggressive defense and overall height advantage kept Miller City's "Three Musketeers" bottled up most of the game. Skip was held to a season-low 8 points. Joe had 7. Frank managed just 4.

But the Wildcats were hardly one dimensional. Defense had become has much a trademark of the team as flashy ball handling and flawless offensive execution. Defense had turned the tide before, and Norris Simpson silently prayed that it would once again.

Skip hounded Gene Schimmoeller from one end of the floor to the other, limiting Ottoville's talented 6-foot-5 center to 10 points, about half his season average. Paul Honigford, Ottoville's other all-league standout, scored 9 points, also under his average.

The lead changed hands 15 times during the contest. Momentum seemed grasped on every basket made, and lost on every basket missed. It was tied 10–10 after one quarter of play. Miller City edged ahead 16–14 at the half, but after three periods, Ottoville was on top 29–27.

The Big Green appeared to take control with a 7–0 run in the second half. But the Wildcats answered with a 9–0 burst of their own.

The game was tied on nine different occasions, the last time at 32–32. It was at that point, though, that Miller City suffered a stunning blow when Skip picked up his fifth and final foul.

Simpson looked down his bench and made a quick decision. Replacing Skip Meyer, Miller City's center, would be Roy Meyer, Skip's 5-5 sophomore brother.

Strategically, replacing your starting center with a pint-sized guard appeared to make no sense. But it's funny how fate often pegs the little things to make the biggest impact. In Roy Meyer's case, destiny demanded it.

All those years going head to head with big brother Skip had forged Roy into a fiery competitor. Lightning quick and daring, he had become as integral a part of Miller City's success as any of the starters.

And in the final minutes of the biggest game of his life, Roy Meyer literally stole victory from the gaping jaws of defeat.

Ottoville had the ball and a chance to take the lead when Roy swooped in, stole a pass and went in for a lay-up.

Roy then committed one of the cardinal sins of Simpson's game plan. After every Miller City basket, Simpson yelled at his players to get back on defense. It was a rule never to be broken. Consequences awaited anyone who did.

After scoring the go-ahead basket, however, Roy faked like he was heading up court, then spun back around, stole the inbounds pass from an unsuspecting Ottoville player, and scored again.

Roy later hit a free throw, completing a game-high 13-point effort. But it was his two stunning steals that sealed the deal for Miller City and earned them their first-ever district championship.

Small as he was, Roy Meyer made a lightweight hero to carry off the floor that memorable night. But he figured he might as well enjoy the ride while it lasted. His daring play may have turned the tide and earned Miller City the district championship. But he also knew that come Monday, when his feet were once again firmly on the ground, they would be running laps for breaking one of Coach Simpson's basic rules.

Norris Simpson, up early as usual, scrounged in the snow-covered bushes outside his apartment for the Republican-Courier.

He'd continued to get his home town newspaper after he had taken the coaching job at Miller City and relocated to Ottawa. Now, if the paper boy could get it on his door step on a consistent basis, he'd be a happy man.

Initially, Simpson just wanted to keep tabs on people and events back home. Lately, not all of the news had been good, and Saturday morning's headlines were especially depressing. Simpson's alma mater—Findlay High—had taken a 20–0 record into the Class A district finals at Bowling Green. But Toledo Woodward's Jim Suszka had tossed in a desperation shot with 2 seconds left to beat the Trojans.

It was like a deja vu sock to the stomach for Simpson. The Trojans had also been 20–0 his senior year at Findlay High. They won the district championship and reached the regional semifinals, but again it was Toledo Woodward that ended their dream season.

Maybe, Simpson thought, his new team—Miller City—could take up the torch for both schools.

As his Wildcats piled win upon win and advanced deeper and deeper in the tournament, Simpson was becoming more and more amazed by the media craze engulfing his team.

Outside of a few pivotal league games, Simpson hadn't even seen a sportswriter during the regular season. The local scribe for the Putnam County Sentinel had been on hand for all of the county tournament games. A few more showed up for the district tournament in Defiance.

Now it seemed a small army of journalists was descending almost daily on the little town of Miller City, grabbing lunch and some of the local flavor at Mac and Rita's, hanging out at Shorty's hoping to find a fresh new angle, popping into practice unannounced and unexpected.

Each writer tried to stamp his own catchy nickname on the team. One called them the Mighty Midgets of Miller City. Another simply hailed them as the Mighty Mites. They were also referred to as the Fabulous Five, the Cinderella Kids, the Miller City Wonders and, in a bit of a religious slap at the predominantly Catholic concentration in the area, the Fisheaters.

Nearly every article centered around the smallness of the town, the school and the players who made up the team. Most detailed the fact that the players had to buy their own shoes, socks and warm-ups, and that the school's gymnasium was little more than a converted barn built years before by the industrial arts class.

Writers unfamiliar with the area went to great lengths explaining how Miller City's boys had to rise before the sun to milk the cows, slop the hogs, gather eggs and feed the livestock before heading off to school. One found ironic joy in the fact that Skip Meyer, the star of the team, had a pet cow named Daisy.

Someone picking up a paper and reading about the Wildcats for the first time would swear they came to school in bib overalls and manure-covered boots.

Simpson chuckled to himself. Ever mindful of any edge, especially a psychological one, he didn't mind the misguided perception of his Wildcats. If opponents wanted to stoke their fragile confidence thinking Miller City was little more than a rag-tag bunch of rubes and hicks, so be it. He knew better.

Simpson had to admit, though, that this group of undersized, overachieving unknowns had surpassed even his grandest dreams.

When he first opened practice four months before, he guessed that, with a lot of work and an equal amount of luck, they might win five or six games. After a decisive win over a strong Leipsic team in January, he'd boasted that, if his team played that well every game, they just might do pretty well in the tournament.

But this, this was something surreal.

Simpson picked up his paper and checked the figures once more. There were 1,200 schools in the state of Ohio that season, 820 in mid- to small-sized Class B division (towns with populations under 2,500), and 380 big schools in Class A. Only 16 teams remained in each division and only one—his—was still undefeated.

That fact merely added to the Miller City mystique.

There was no denying it. The Wildcats were quickly becoming the Cinderella story of the 1950 basketball tournament, and everybody loves a fairy tale in the making.

But this fairy tale also had a big, nasty ogre, and the name of this giant was Delphos St. John's.

Four district champions would square off in the Class B regional tournament to be played at the University of Toledo Fieldhouse. Miller City (25–0) and Delphos St. John's (27–1) would meet in the first game; Leesville (18–3) and Troy-Lucky (20–2) in the second.

Realistically, most fans of Northwest Oho basketball figured only one of those teams was a shoo-in to advance to state.

Delphos St. John's was not only ranked N0.1 in the state that season, the Blue Jays were also the defending Class B state champions.

St. John's had already played 28 games and won 27 of them. The only loss was to Toledo Central Catholic, a strong Class A program.

The Blue Jays returned four seniors from their state championship team, including two of the top players in Ohio in Dick Honigford, a 6-foot-7, 240-pound center who averaged 30 points a game, and Ralph Wagner, a sharp-shooting 5–11 guard. Both had been named to the all-tournament team the year before when St. John's beat Lockland Wayne 47–43 in the Class B state championship game.

Simpson didn't need a newspaper article to find that information, though. For most of the 1949–50 season, he had been keenly aware of the brooding juggernaut sitting just across the Putnam County line, like a marauding army hunkered down on the very border of the basketball kingdom his Wildcats had claimed as their own.

But there was more to the story than even the most dogged sportswriters had been able to ferret out.

Simpson also knew that Miller City and Delphos St. John's, first-time first-round opponents in the Class B regional, were supposed to have met during the regular season. The game had been on the original schedule. But before the season even started, Superintendent Ferd Ball informed Simpson that Delphos St. John's had bought its way out of the contract, reportedly for a $250 fee. The reason, according to Ball, was that St. John's officials had said they wanted to free up dates on the schedule to play "tougher competition."

So be it, Simpson thought. Not that his team needed any more incentive than the fact they were playing the N0.1-ranked team in the state. But that little tidbit might become a handy bit of bulletin board bait, and at this stage of the game you looked for any motivational edge you could find.

Norris Simpson felt himself sinking through an endless realm of darkness, layer upon silent layer, each one quieter, it seemed, and more desolate than the one before.

He felt himself drifting, an aimless presence in a vast void.

It was peaceful, so very, very peaceful.

Something, though, was pulling him back.

"Coach!"

The sound anchored him, gave him bearing.

"Coach! Are you okay?"

The darkness was being sucked away, like nothingness into a black hole.

"Coach Simpson! Say something."

He felt the presence, then, of people around him.

Then he heard the noise, starting low and growing ever louder. It was like walking through the door of a soundproof room onto the platform of a train station just as a speeding freight went barreling by.

"Coach. You okay?"

Gradually, Simpson recognized Charlie Warnimont, Miller City's team manager, steadying him with a hand on his shoulder.

The firm grip on his other arm, he soon learned, belonged to Dick Krauss, his volunteer assistant who that day had been the color man for Dick Davies' radio broadcast of the Class B regional semifinals.

"What happened?"

Superintendent Ferd Ball had come running up, his tie askew, his face beet red, a look of genuine concern on his face.

Had it been a dream? Was it real?

Up on his feet now, Simpson looked out onto the floor at the University of Toledo Fieldhouse where a delirious bunch of skinny players in rag-tag uniforms was whooping and hollering in a sea of blue-clad fans on the UT court.

It came back to Simpson in a flash—the game, the tip, the final frantic seconds.

He stole a glance at the clock on the fieldhouse wall. All zeroes.

And the bright glowing numbers on either side of the clock said it all—Miller City 43, Delphos St. John's 42.

Simpson's Mighty Mites had done it. Before a standing room only crowd of over 6,000 screaming fans and fanatics, they had pulled off the upset no one thought possible.

They had beaten the defending state champions, the N0.1-ranked team in the state, the team many felt could have written its name on the gold state tournament trophy when the season began those many, many months ago.

Suddenly swept up in the crowd of back-slappers and hand-pumpers, Simpson struggled to put it all into perspective.

He remembered the missed foul shots—oh, how he hated missed free throws—that could have put his team ahead with under 20 seconds to play. But Skip Meyer—Mr. Clutch throughout the tournament—somehow wriggled in among the giants and tipped in the rebound.

Delphos would have its chance as well. But destiny had seemingly taken the Wildcats under her wing. The shot did not fall, there was a scramble for the loose ball, and then the horn sounded.

The rest was a blur. All the ecstasy, the emotion, the euphoria of the moment welled up in Simpson like a tidal wave and overwhelmed him. With bedlam breaking loose all around him, Norris Simpson fainted dead away.

Simpson would for years be a tad embarrassed by the incident. He needn't have been. The game, from the opening tip until the final horn, had not been one for the faint-hearted.

Twelve times the score was deadlocked. The lead changed hands 17 times.

Simpson had expected Delphos St. John's to look to its big guns—Honigford and Wagner—early on. And the Blue Jays didn't disappoint him.

Poised, prepared and brimming with confidence, St. John's quickly went to work, opening a 10–6 first-quarter lead with Honigford's inside strength and Wagner's deadly accuracy from the outside leading the way.

But like a hungry bulldog, Miller City clamped onto the Blue Jays and hung tough. Mixing things up, Simpson called out a different number—the codes for his various defenses—almost every time down the floor, forcing the Blue Jays to make constant adjustments. Sometimes they faced a 1–3–1 zone, sometimes a 2–3. At times, it appeared Miller City was employing a box-and-one on Honigford, and always there was the tenacious trapping pressure that made every mistake costly.

Simpson had assigned Skip Meyer the monumental task of trying to stop Honigford, but he realized one man could not do it alone. So Simpson tag-teamed the Blue Jays' giant, double-teaming Honigford with Skip's quickness and Dick Barlage's bulk every chance they could.

Simpson knew he could not shut Honigford down, not entirely anyway. But hopefully they could contain him and keep the all-state big man from becoming a one-man wrecking crew inside the paint.

Out on the perimeter, Frank Schroeder was bird-dogging Wagner as well, hounding him at every turn, denying every pass, contesting every shot.

Gradually, the pressure took a toll. Miller City crept back within a basket (21–19) by the half, then staged a strong third quarter to go up 31–28.

Honigford banked one in off the glass to open the fourth quarter, however, and Wagner connected from outside. Frank's aggressive defensive play on Wagner finally cost him his fifth foul, and he headed to the bench. But Roy Meyer, the sophomore spark plug who had played such a huge role in the tournament, came in, converted a quick basket and put Miller City back in front.

Wagner then answered for Delphos, and when two of the Blue Jays' other veterans—Jim Etter and Dick Youngpeter—scored, St. John's regained the lead at 38–36.

But Miller City had some clutch players, too. Junior McDonald hit a free throw and Roy Meyer his second basket of the final period. When Skip scored, the Wildcats led 41–38 with 1:10 on the clock.

Big-time players make big-time plays, though. Honigford, held to just four baskets the entire second half by Meyer and Barlage, powered his way inside for a lay-in and Wagner, limited to a single field goal by Schroeder, followed a Miller City miss with two free throws as Delphos stormed back in front, 42–41.

With all 6,000 fans on their feet, Miller City went back on offense. St. John's Coach Frank Sowecke had warned his players that the Wildcats would probably go to their money man, Skip Meyer, in the clutch and to double team him if possible. But that left Dick Barlage free for just a second, and the stocky senior was fouled putting up a shot.

Overall, Miller City was an excellent free throw shooting team.

The Wildcats had even won the trophy at the annual Putnam County free throw shooting competition.

But in the pressure-packed cauldron of a regional tournament game against the N0.1-ranked defending state champions, with victory or defeat just 15 feet away, even the bravest man can flinch.

Barlage's first shot went up.

A miss.

And now that pressure had increased tenfold.

Another shot.

Another miss.

In a heartbeat, though, quick beat big.

St. John's had the size, and the inside position.

But Miller City had quick, and in the blink of an eye, Skip Meyer slashed in among the giants, stretched as far as he could reach and got just enough of the ball to tip it up, up, up and in.

It is amazing more people in the standing room only crowd did not keel over as their emotions swung drastically from one extreme to another.

But the drama was not yet over.

Delphos St. John's still had a few precious seconds left on the clock. And a team as tournament-tested as the Blue Jays knew best how to use them.

Quickly setting up a play, St. John's hurried the ball up court. But before a shot could be launched, another whistle blew. This time the foul was on Miller City, and now it was Delphos that would have to answer to a demon named "Pressure."

The player stepping to the line was named Johnny Clark, but it may not have mattered. On those momentous occasions when destiny seems to be following a predestined script, it is not so much the names of the individual characters themselves as much as it is the physical space they occupy that gives credence to the storyline.

If Miller City's mystical, magical season was to continue, there was but one outcome. And when Clark's free throw bounced out and not in during those final unbelievable seconds, it was as if destiny had tapped Cinderella on the shoulder and asked her if she could stick around a little longer and dance at least one more dance.

In the bowels of the University of Toledo Fieldhouse, in a locker room beneath the crowded stands that rocked and thundered from 12,000 stomping feet, Norris Simpson scanned the faces of the young men before him.

He liked what he saw.

Above their little huddle loomed all the dangerous influences coaches strive to keep away from their players, things like uncertainty and apprehension, worry and fret, indecision and overzealous bravado. Those attributes are ever the curse of the true fan who knows deep inside that he can never dictate the outcome of a contest, only observe it.

But down below, all was calm.

An outsider might have been stunned by the composure of the little group. Didn't they realize that a regional championship was at stake? Were they not aware that a bid to the pinnacle of all high school sports—the state tournament—was on the line?

The man in the melon-orange shirt and the neat grey suit wasn't surprised, though.

Simpson had seen his Cinderella team overcome huge deficits and overwhelming odds just to get this far, and they hadn't done it by going into a panic every time things got a little hairy.

True, the first half of their regional showdown with Leesville had not been their best basketball of the season. Maybe it was the timing.

Creatures of routine, Simpson's players were used to getting up at dawn, taking care of their chores, breaking for lunch when the dinner bell rang promptly at noon. If they did have a chance to play a little basketball in the middle of a Saturday afternoon, it was usually for an impromptu pick-up game or a quick round of H-O-R-S-E, definitely not a regional tournament battle.

Simpson also knew that at this stage of the game, you were playing everybody else's best of the best. And Leesville, 19–3 and the Crawford County tournament champion, was wearing that label proudly.

Right from the start, the Wildcats seemed a bit off. They were doing well on the boards, but their shooting, usually a strength of the team, was inconsistent.

The teams traded baskets early, but neither could pull away. It was tied 8–8 late in the first quarter, then 10–10. Joe Lammers beat the buzzer to put Miller City on top 14–10 at the break. But Leesville, coached by Bob Morrison, a Findlay College graduate like Simpson, fought back in the second quarter to go up 21–20. Skip Meyer's free throw just before the half sent the teams into to the locker rooms tied at 23.

There were times when Simpson's insides felt like a bag of bowling balls tumbling down a steep flight of stairs. On the sidelines, he was a whirlwind in constant motion. But in the quiet confines of that locker room he was composed. It was time to strategize, not rant and rave. And in the faces of his players he saw reassurance, not panic.

"Boys," Simpson said in that low, even tone of his, "they had their chance in the first half. Now it's ours. We're going to press the snot out of them in the second half and see if they can stand the pressure."

Two teams stood dead even when the third quarter began. Eight frantic minutes later, it was all but over.

Miller City fans knew what to expect. They'd seen firsthand the devastation Simpson's defensive schemes could cause. But the rest of the 6,000 fans in the University of Toledo Fieldhouse were left in awe.

Pressing from one end of the floor to the other, trapping at every chance, hounding every possession with man-to-man and match-up zone defense, Miller City's Wildcats went after Leesville like, well, like wildcats.

Hit with a defensive haymaker from the second half tip, Leesville never survived Miller City's suffocating attack. Every mistake—and there were several—became a lost opportunity for Leesville and a golden opportunity for Miller City.

Turnovers became fast-break transition baskets as the Wildcats went up by two points, then four, then six and then eight.

Sportswriters covering the game would herald Miller City's 18–5 edge in the third quarter as the turning point in the game. The astute ones focused their articles on a defense that limited Leesville to just one field goal and three free throws the entire third quarter.

Almost lost in Miller City's second-half blitz was the play of Dick Barlage. Morrison had obviously told Leesville's players to concentrate on Skip Meyer, the Wildcats' standout who had had a big first half for Miller City. But that left the other big guy open, and Barlage took advantage. Held without a basket or free throw the entire first half, he scored all 12 of his points in the game's final 16 minutes.

Skip would finish with a game-high 21 points. Joe Lammers had 13, Frank Schroeder 8 and Roy Meyer 5.

Leesville also had good offensive balance. But in the end, it wasn't quite enough for the little school on the banks of the Sandusky River. Leesville did play Miller City to a standoff in the fourth quarter. But by then the Wildcats were nursing a 10-to-14-point lead.

Every few seconds, Norris Simpson cast an anxious glance at a Toledo Fieldhouse clock.

Could it possibly run any slower?

But as Miller City's lead grew, so to did the realization that this team, his team, was going to be making the trip every team in the state of Ohio wanted to make.

This rag-tag collection of small-town farm boys in their ratty uniforms and tattered shoes, this scrawny group of undersized overachievers who never realized they weren't supposed to be this good, this pint-sized team with more heart and hustle than bone and muscle, this team was going to the state tournament.

As the horn sounded on Miller City's 60–46 victory, the players rushed to the bench, hoisted their rookie head coach on their scrawny shoulders, and began parading around the gym.

"Man," Simpson thought to himself for only about the 1,200th time that season. "This is going to be one heckuva ride."

"Our father, who art in heaven, hallowed be thy name. . . ."

Sitting in the middle seat of the Nash station wagon that Coach Simpson had "borrowed" to cart his team to tournament games, Frank Schroeder prayed like he had never prayed before.

Skip Meyer sat on his left. Joe Lammers on his right.

They were praying, too.

Dick Barlage and Junior McDonald, the other two starters on Miller City's team, were in the back with Roy Meyer, Skip's younger brother, and Vern Schroeder. Not far behind, in a second car, Fr. Herman Lammers and Superintendent Ferd Ball followed with the rest of the team. Then came the cheerleaders and Ike Conkright, who had re-painted his car in the blue and gold school colors, leading a lengthy caravan of fans.

The Miller City Wildcats, as unlikely a final four team as any in Ohio basketball history, were heading for the state tournament in Columbus. And in every vehicle in the caravan, it's a good bet the "Our Fathers" and "Hail Marys" were coming fast and furious as rosary beads passed like golden nuggets through white-knuckled fingers.

Frank's mind raced as he mumbled the prayers he'd long ago memorized as a child. How had the years flown by so fast?

The two young men flanking him could probably fill in the gaps. They'd been beside him all along, from the time they started school at New Cleveland and first started shooting hoops on the blacktopped playground.

Heck, they could hardly get the ball to the rim back then.

But they grew, and as they did, so did their passion for this game. At first, it was just pick-up games among classmates. By fourth and fifth-grade, they had organized teams with organized practices.

This group thrived on competition, though. So Fr. Sylvester Schmelzer, pastor of the Holy Family Catholic Church at New Cleveland, got them into a CYO league and began carting them around.

Frank thought back to those many road trips—seven, sometimes eight kids packed into Fr. Schmelzer's car as they headed for any small town or out-of-the-way place where they could get up a game or enter a tournament.

It was a rule of Fr. Schmelzer's that they say the rosary along the way. He was sure it would strengthen their religious zeal and, perhaps, bring them good fortune. Behind his back, the young boys snickered that, because of Fr. Schmelzer's driving, the good fortune would be if they survived the trip.

They moved up a notch in junior high, sometimes getting to take the floor before the JV and varsity match-ups when schools, figuring they had to fire up the boilers anyway, played three games back-to-back-to-back. That merely fueled the dreams that had been growing in all of them for some time now.

Dreams are the fairy tales that sustain us until childhood reluctantly slips away. What young boy—alone on a basketball court, a ball diamond, an open field—hasn't seen himself making the game-winning shot, hitting the game-winning home run, scoring the game-winning touchdown against the mightiest of foes? Could it be anything less?

Specifics—as pliable as the imagination would allow—didn't matter. Miss a 30-footer? Pop up? Fumble? No! There was a foul and you're going to the line. The pop-up was dropped and you get one more chance. The fumble bounces wildly back to you and you run, run, run for the end zone.

You see, dreams, like fairy tales, must have a happy ending. If they don't, they become something sinister. They become reality.

"Hail Mary, full of grace, the Lord is with you. . . ."

Frank realized that perhaps it was the brooding presence of reality that had been troubling him since he'd loaded his gym bag in the trunk of Simpson's Nash station wagon on an overcast March morning for the long trip to Columbus. Throughout his entire career, the state basketball tournament had been a dream, like a golden ring on the top of a mountain so tall you felt you could never reach the top.

Back home, shooting hoops against the barn, he knew how that dream ended. But this was reality, and this was something his well-intentioned imagination could not control.

For one, he never could have imagined that the teams he'd face in the state tournament would have names like Corning and Eaton and Geneva. After some difficulty, he'd found them on a map and made a mental note of where they were located in the state.

Coach Simpson had pinned a newspaper article up in his class-room with more details. Corning, Miller City's opponent in the semifinals, was from Perry County. The team had a huge record—25–4—and, by comparison, a huge enrollment. Heck, the district probably had as many boys in its senior class as Miller City had in the entire school.

Corning? Never in all his glorious dreams had Frank imagined himself playing a team called Corning. But the team fit the mold of any opponent he had ever conjured up. They were big. They were fast. They were talented.

Maybe the ghostly teams in his dreams had just been waiting for some substance. And now they had it.

Frank was suddenly aware of rosaries being cupped and pocketed as the prayers came to a close. He moved to put his away as well, then hesitated.

Maybe, he thought, a few more "Our Fathers" and "Hail Marys" wouldn't hurt.

Norris Simpson stood at the blackboard in a locker room under the stands of the Fairgrounds Coliseum in Columbus.

Diagramming plays, Simpson punctuated each and every screech of the chalk with a booming tirade of Miller City's play in the first half of the Class B state semifinal against Corning.

But Joe Lammers didn't hear a word he said.

Sitting alone, off to one side, Joe cradled his head in his hands, shutting out all but his own inner thoughts.

No one was pointing fingers. That wasn't the nature of this team.

But in his mind, Joe was shouldering much of the blame for what had been one of the Wildcats' worst first halves of the season. They trailed Corning's Railroaders 30–22 and only a late second-quarter rally had kept the game from being a blow out.

Before an overflow crowd of over 7,100, Corning was living up to all the pre-tournament hype and hoopla. Tall and talented, the Railroaders had averaged over 62 points a game during the season with a backboard sweeping, fast-breaking offense that definitely liked to run the floor.

Corning had scored off the opening tip, ran up a 5–2 lead before Simpson called a time out, then went up 16–6 with an 11–4 burst.

Skip Meyer ended a five-possession drought for Miller City with a tip-in to cut the deficit to 16–8 by the end of the quarter. But Corning's big guns—Jerry Roof and Bill Thiessen—fueled another surge in the second period as the Railroaders increased the lead to 21–9 on a short jump shot, 23–11 when Roof banked one in, and finally 25–11 on a fast-break lay-up.

Despite being the only undefeated team left in the state (27–0), Miller City's Wildcats had quickly become the sentimental favorites of the state tournament. Part of that was due to the Columbus newspapers, who cranked out story after story about the ragamuffin band of farm boys in the ratty uniforms from a tiny hamlet up north who had to buy their own socks and warm-ups and who played their home games in a gymnasium dubbed "The Barn." They had to milk the cows and slop the hogs and feed the chickens, but they also played the game of basketball in a mystical, almost magical way that rekindled memories of the wondrous Waterloo Wonders of the 1930s.

All it took was for someone to holler "They look more like a junior high team," as they filed into the Coliseum, and they had immediately become the spunky-little-brother favorites in the hearts of anyone who had come to the state tournament unhindered by pre-determined school loyalties.

Some were beginning to think, though, that Cinderella may have stayed at the ball too long.

Corning obviously deserved much of the credit for its first-half success. The bigger school was stocked with good athletes, good basketball players, and it showed in their play.

Maybe Corning Mayor Sam Frazier was right. Approached by a reporter before the game and asked for his prediction, he replied, "It's in the bag."

The half-time scoreboard didn't dispute that.

It wasn't as if Miller City's players were dumbstruck by the situation or their surroundings. All through the tournament people seeing the Wildcats for the first time had been most impressed by their poise, their cool demeanor in the face of any adversity, their single-minded refusal to crack under intense pressure.

One of the most telling examples of the Wildcats' composure came during time outs. While opposing teams stood and huddled around their head coach, Miller City's players simply sprawled on the floor like children at play seeking a bit of relief from a hot afternoon sun.

True, when they had come to Columbus earlier in the week for their scheduled practice at the Coliseum, they had been in awe of the mammoth facility. Empty, dark and foreboding, their footsteps rang loudly off distant walls. To them, most of whom had rarely ventured beyond the county lines before that season, it must have seemed like walking into the Grand Canyon at twilight, when the booming echoes only enhanced the size and the immensity of the place.

But now the stands were packed to capacity. Every seat was taken, and the Wildcats had played to standing-room-only crowds before.

No. Something else was afoot. Simpson was saying as much as he stood at the blackboard and did what he did best—formulate a plan, instill confidence, and most of all, get his players to believe they could achieve anything if they played as he knew they could.

Joe heard the words, but he wasn't really listening.

No one individual could be faulted for Miller City's sub-par first half. But Joe felt he was to blame. As a senior and a veteran, he should be leading by example. He'd had a few turnovers in the first half, though. He'd been burned a time or two on defense, and when he picked up his third foul midway through the second quarter, he spent the last few minutes of the first half on the bench.

But it was his shooting that bothered him most. He'd always

been one of the best outside shots on the team. From the time as a small boy when he had taped an oatmeal box to the laundry room door and used a balled-up wad of socks for a ball he'd always been able to put it through the hoop.

But now he felt like he was chucking pumpkins at a thimble.

He had no excuses. The backboards at the Fairgrounds Coliseum were clear glass, something Miller City's players had not seen before. But Simpson, in a move as strategic as any in state tournament history, drew on his own experiences in tournament play and the savvy of his old high school coach. Claiming his players would be at a distinct disadvantage, he petitioned officials to cover the glass. They consented, and taped white paper over the back of the backboards.

Corning, though, had had no problems shooting the ball in the first half.

"That was the problem," Simpson was saying as his voice, rising now, brought Joe and the rest of the players to a sudden alertness. "Offensively, they do a lot of the same things we do. Only they've been doing it better.

"We're going to press them and turn up the defensive pressure in the second half. We have to make them earn everything they get.

"They've had their turn. Not it's ours."

Simpson's words were still ringing in their ears as the Wildcats huddled one last time before the second-half tip. But it was Simpson's final comment to him that stuck with Joe Lammers.

"Take the shot, Joe," he'd said as he sent his players onto the floor. "If it's there, don't be afraid to take it."

Miller City had ended the first half with an 8–2 run to at least make the score respectable. In the first few seconds of the second half, Frank Schroeder made it more than that.

When the Wildcat's press forced a quick Corning turnover, Frank, always a spark plug for the team, converted a driving lay-up and was fouled. He missed the free throw, but when Skip tipped the rebound back to him, Frank drove into the lane and banked in a mid-range leaner.

Corning got on the board on Dick Garrison's foul shot. But Miller City answered right back when Joe, open in the right corner, launched a long set shot that hit nothing but the bottom of the net.

"Just like throwing socks through the oatmeal box," he mused as he headed back on defense.

Roof's 3-point play quieted the Miller City fans in a hurry, and could have signaled a huge swing in momentum.

But Skip tipped in a miss on the other end, and Junior McDonald nailed a free throw after another Corning turnover.

The Wildcats, seemingly done for when they trailed by 14 points in the second quarter, were suddenly back within one.

Maybe Cinderella wasn't done dancing after all.

With Simpson popping off the bench on every possession, Miller City forced still another turnover, and Joe, his confidence restored, nailed a 22-footer from the right corner to give Miller City its first lead of the game, 35–34.

Joe then hit another set shot from the exact same spot, Skip made a foul shot, and Frank followed with a free throw and a basket. When Corning extended the defense to cover Joe on the wing, he drove the middle for a reverse lay-up, capping an 11–0 run that put Miller City on top 43–34 with 1:43 left in the third quarter.

Theissen ended Corning's drought with a free throw. But Miller City's scintillating 20–5 run in the third quarter had turned the tide.

Corning would rally. The Railroaders were too talented and too determined a team not to. A 7–2 run in the fourth quarter would get them back within four of the Wildcats, 46–42. But destiny would not have been satisfied, nor history met, if Miller City had stumbled then.

Utilizing their outstanding ball handling ability and the rules of the time, the Wildcats worked the ball until someone was fouled, then calmly made the first free throw and took the ball out of bounds.

As the big clock on the Coliseum scoreboard wound down tick by excruciating tick, Miller City stretched the lead to five points, then six, then seven.

Then suddenly it was over. And for just a split second, Norris Simpson and his players stared up at 53–45 final on the scoreboard and wondered yet again if it was really real.

It was.

Victory had touched them once again. Twenty-eight times they had stepped onto the floor, and 28 times they had triumphed. Just one game separated them from a perfect season and a state championship.

Four months ago, even they could not have dreamed such a lofty goal was possible. But now anything and everything seemed within the reach of an unlikely bunch of rag-tag farm kids who simply could not—would not—accept defeat.

Al Haft was getting ready to turn out the lights and lock up when a small caravan of cars pulled into his parking lot. As owner/operator of the Haft Motel, Al didn't like late arrivals. It just meant more work and a later bed time for him.

But things had been a bit slow lately, and something about this little group intrigued him, especially the two men who climbed out of the first car and walked up to the door. One was a smallish man in a hound's-tooth hat. The other, a string bean of a man, towered over him by a good foot-and-a-half.

"Can I help you gentlemen?" Al asked as they approached the counter.

"We were wondering," the smaller man said, "if you had a few rooms to put us and our boys up for a night or two?"

"You guys a ball team or something?"

"I'm Ferd Ball," the smaller man said. "This here is Coach Simpson, and we're—"

"Wait a minute. You're those Miller City boys aren't you?" Al said. "I was listening to the state tournament games on my Philco in the office back there, and I heard how you boys came back after being 14 points down and beat that Corning team."

A fan of all high school sports, Al never missed the state basketball tournament, even if it meant just listening to the games on the radio.

"That was a mighty big win for you boys," he was saying. "And you got a mighty big chore ahead of you in Saturday's final. I hear that Eaton team is awful good. Heck, they're almost a Class A-size school. And that big kid of theirs—I think his name is Neff—he's all-state. He's big time."

"I guess we'll just have to worry about that when the time comes," said Simpson. "Right now we just need to get the boys settled in somewhere. Can you put us up?"

"Can do," Al said with a smile. "I wish you guys would've called ahead first, though, so I could've had the rooms ready."

"That would have been nice," Ball said as he stepped to the counter and began to sign in. "But we really didn't have that option. We like to think our boys can win every time they step on the floor. But it being the state tournament, you never know what can happen. And these boys, well, they're counted on to do a lot of things back home. If we'd lost, they'd be halfway home by now so they could get up in the morning for chores."

"I know what you mean," said Al, who dabbled in a little farming himself.

"Well, let's get them boys inside and set them up in some rooms. They can hang out here tomorrow and be all rested for that big game Saturday. Then we'll see if ol' Al's magic works again."

"How's that?" Ball asked.

"Well, last year about this time, another team came in here looking for a place to stay," Al said. "The team was Hamilton, and you know what they did, don't you?"

Ferd Ball, the superintendent, didn't. But Norris Simpson, the basketball coach, did.

"Yeah," Simpson said, a slow smile crossing his face. "They won the state championship."

There is, in every major confrontation, a moment, a single second of time, when destiny shakes her bony fist and lets fly the tumbling chances of fate.

Wars can be won or lost in that mere moment. Thrones can be salvaged or lost.

It is that split second before David unloosed the stone.

Victory hangs in the balance, waiting for the scales to be tipped by the gravitational pull of greatness.

Defeat can be but a tick away.

It is but a moment. But for Norris Simpson and his Miller City Wildcats, that moment was becoming an eternity.

Nearly 9,000 fans in the Columbus Fairgrounds Coliseum were none too happy about it, either.

Boos cascaded down in waves from all corners of the arena as an overflow crowd, packed to the rafters thanks to the number of counterfeit tickets sold in the parking lot, waited to see if history would be made that warm March day in the spring of 1950.

Everyone who could beg, borrow or steal a ticket into the Class B final had come to see if the little school from up north could cap off one of the most amazing seasons in Ohio high school basketball history by winning a state championship.

The match-up was the stuff of legend and lore.

The sentimental favorite was Miller City. Just 37 boys in the entire high school. Only two starters 6-foot or taller. Uniforms so tattered and faded they looked like they got them on sale at a thrift store.

State tournament veterans who over the years had seen the best teams in the state come and go were intrigued. On outward appearances, this group looked no better than a good junior high team. But after seeing the teamwork, the ball handling, the hustle and execution of the Wildcats, even they had to admit that it spoke to the basketball purist in all their souls.

But those basketball purists were well aware that sentimental favorites often get chewed up and spit out by teams like Eaton, especially in the pressure cooker that is the state tournament.

One of the biggest schools in the Class B division, Eaton was nearly five times the size of Miller City. The Eagles, who had won the 1948 state title, were looking for their second crown in three years, and with Gene Neff, their 6–5 all-state center leading the way, they had manhandled a good Geneva team 56–41 in the semifinals.

Eaton fans were expecting an easy time in the final as well. What they got, though, was a quick, scrappy Miller City team that, instead of backing down from the big guys inside, challenged them with slashing drives to the basket.

The Wildcats did not shoot well in the first quarter. But they drew fouls on Eaton's big men, scored their first six points from the line, and led 6–4 midway through the first period. Skip then scored in the lane, and Joe hit a shot from outside as Miller City went up 10–6.

Eaton fans sat in stunned disbelief. But not for long.

The Eagles had too much talent to be denied, and too much tournament experience to become flustered. With Miller City packing its defense tight inside, the Eagles got two long set shots from the perimeter to forge a 10–10 tie at the break.

Miller City went up 12–10 when Junior hit a runner in the lane, 15–14 when Frank knocked one down from the perimeter, and 18–17 when Skip scored inside.

The Eagles then flexed their considerable muscles.

With Neff leading the assault, Eaton finished the second quarter with a 10–5 run. That not only gave the Eagles a 27–23 lead at the half, it also seemed to send a resounding message throughout the Coliseum as to who was the better team.

In a quiet Miller City locker room, Simpson sensed not a hint of despair in his team. That didn't surprise him. Of the many attributes he had used to describe his team—to fellow coaches, to outsiders seeing his players for the first time, to the scribes who would document their season—it was the unflappable calmness of his boys in the face of staggering obstacles and adversity that he mentioned most.

That, he felt, was the truest mark of their character.

Beyond those thick concrete walls, there were many who did not share that thought. As the second half approached and fans scuttled back to their seats, there was a growing confidence among the Eaton faithful and a growing concern among the rest.

No one could question the spunk and gritty determination of the Miller City five. But everyone there had seen the explosive power of an Eaton team that could score points in bunches. Eaton had played an inconsistent first half. But their burst right before the intermission was proof that when the Eagles put their complete game together, they could absolutely dominate.

All it would take, everyone knew, was a similar run to begin the second half, and it would not be a matter of *if*, but for *how long*, the undersized, outmanned underdogs of Miller City could hang on.

As the two teams aligned themselves at center court for the second half tip, there was that split second in time when fate and destiny were locked in that tug-o-war stalemate.

But that decisive split second got stuck in a time warp.

The big clock on the Coliseum scoreboard continued to run, tick by tick by tick. But the battle being played out before it came to a sudden standstill.

Destiny would be delayed. Fate would just have to sit and wait.

When Eaton gained possession of the ball, the Eagles did the one thing no one could possibly expect them to do—they stalled.

With its guards perched out high, almost at mid-court, Eaton was content to simply stand and hold the ball. Not for a few seconds to try and force Miller City out of its tight zone. Not for a minute to see how the Wildcats would react.

Eaton stalled the entire third quarter.

Perhaps Eaton Coach Gene Ellington was well aware that the third quarter was usually the time when Miller City slapped on its vaunted press, and he wanted to deny them the strategy that had turned so many games their way before.

Perhaps he felt comfortable with his four-point lead, figuring that Miller City couldn't score if it never touched the ball.

His explanation after the game offered another option.

"We were four points ahead and four of our players had three fouls," Ellington would say later. "I wanted to stall through the period to keep my boys in the game for the big final period, when I was sure we could win. If I had it to do over again, I'd play it the same way."

Simpson was at first stunned by Eaton's tactics. But he, too, was willing to take a risk. His Wildcats weren't making any headway, but they weren't losing ground, either.

"We agreed to let them play with the ball until about a minute was left," he said later. "And then we were going out after it."

And so the last two teams remaining in the Class B state tournament stood toe-to-toe—although at a respectable distance—as one stalemated minute melted into two, then into three and four and five.

For a time, it seemed as if the entire third quarter of the state championship game would come and go without so much as a sneaker squeak to know it had ever really been played. But as the game clock clicked under two minutes left in the period, Frank, who had made a few half-hearted feints to the outside, forced a turnover that the Wildcats converted on the other end.

Another turnover in the final seconds of the quarter and two free throws by Joe just before the buzzer tacked two more points on the board.

Eaton had not attempted a single shot the entire period. Miller City hadn't had many opportunities, either. But the Wildcats took advantage of the few they did get. With one quarter to play, the deficit was down to a single point, 28–27.

Long would fans discuss Eaton's choice to stall away the third quarter. Many would claim it changed the whole complexion of the game.

Who can say? In the final analysis, maybe the stall didn't change destiny that day. Maybe it only delayed it.

Energized by its third-quarter run and well rested Miller City went on the offensive. Skip had been quiet throughout the third quarter. But he scored the first five points of the fourth period, converting two free throws, then a basket inside, and connecting from the line once again to put Miller City up 32–28 with six minutes left in the game.

Eaton then got the surge Ellington expected. The Eagles' all-state standout led the charge, with Neff scoring three points during a 5–0 run. It was his free throw that put his team back on top 33–32.

Simpson then called a strategic time out, essentially to give his battered players a rest but also to remind them how close they were to achieving their dream.

The pep talk paid off.

Vern Schroeder hit a clutch basket off the bench to put Miller City back in front, and Skip hit two free throws. On their next trip down the floor, Joe slashed in from the weak side, took a pass from Skip out front, and scored again.

With 2:45 left, the Wildcats nursed a 38–33 lead.

Neff then showcased his all-Ohio talent, scoring a basket and adding a free throw to bring the Eagles back within two, 38–36, with his 17th point of the game.

Simpson used another time out to calm his troops, then made his own bold move. When the Wildcats took the floor, they took a page from Eaton's own playbook.

This time, Miller City stalled.

Now it was Eaton that needed to force something—a bad pass, a poor shot, a turnover of any kind.

But the Eagles were dealing with a team that had beaten 28 straight opponents by never beating itself.

With time ticking down, the Eagles eventually had to foul. But Miller City made sure the ball was always in the hands of the right guy when that happened.

Skip's foul shot gave Miller City a three-point cushion—39–36. Under the rules of the day, the Wildcats could shoot one free throw, then take the ball out bounds. It fell into a kind of rhythm then—free throw, possession, free throw, possession—as each point became a statement in itself in the 44–36 victory.

Skip Meyer made all eight of his free throws in the fourth quarter, and a state record 12 of 12 for the game. He scored 16 points, Frank Schroeder added 15 and Joe Lammers finished with 6 for Miller City, which converted 22 of 33 free throws overall and out-scored Eaton 22–10 from the line.

Those statistical specifics were all lost in the moment, though. When the clock finally showed nothing but zeroes, a couple thousand fans who had come to embrace a tiny town and the unbeatable spirit its basketball team embodied stormed the Fairgrounds Coliseum floor to hoist upon their shoulders a bold rookie coach and a scrappy bunch of young men who had turned a dream into reality.

EPILOGUE

As a long serpentine caravan of vehicles wound its way north from Columbus, Norris Simpson sat in the front seat of the lead car and twirled a simple treasure in his long, strong fingers.

It was Sunday, the morning after his underdog Miller City Wildcats had pulled off one of the most amazing feats in Ohio prep basketball history by winning the Class B state championship. Behind him sat his players, mumbling their prayers as they said the rosary. Nestled between his team captains—Frank Schroeder and Skip Meyer—was the championship trophy.

Simpson was holding something he considered just as precious, a net from the state championship game. Everything had been a blur in the madhouse that was the Fairgrounds Coliseum following Miller City's 44–36 victory over Eaton. Ecstatic fans rushed the floor, trophy presentations had to be made, sportswriters clamored for his thoughts and feelings about his team's 29–0 season and the improbable state championship that capped it off.

It was only later, as he was leaving the locker room with his team, that a man he had never seen before stopped him and handed him the net.

"You might want to keep this," the man said, "for a souvenir."

The man was Elwood Pitzer, and a few hours after Miller City's stirring victory in the Class B final, Pitzer would lead his Springfield team to a 53–48 win over Akron South in the Class A championship match-up. Pitzer had been at the earlier game and noticed that, in all the hoopla and commotion following Miller City's win, the Wildcats had forgotten the tradition of cutting down the nets.

"I have to remember," Simpson, thought to himself, "to send that man a thank you."

A stickler for detail, Simpson tried to analyze the past few months in a concise, systematic manner. It was his nature.

But it all seemed so surreal now, like trying to recall a dream he wasn't sure he'd really had.

He'd had no grandiose plans when he'd first opened practice four months, five months, an eternity ago.

The collection of athletes that turned out made it apparent any optimism within him would be guarded at best. They were small. And fundamentally, they were rough.

So he worked them. Hard.

But these were farm boys used to hard work. And they responded, just as hard.

Initially, Simpson felt they'd be lucky to win a handful of games. But as the victories began to pile up, so too did his expectations.

Each game became more than a simple 32-minute exhibition of offensive sets and defensive styles. Instead, each game became an example of what heart and desire and determination—coupled with the right training and enthusiasm—can really accomplish.

Each and every game became a testament that it is not the size of the man but his will to succeed that determines his fate.

Simpson could think of a number of times when that truth had been tested—the games against Ottoville and Leipsic, the pre-season favorites to win the league; the district win over Archbold; the regional semifinal win over Delphos St. John's; the state tournament wins over opponents much bigger in size and reputation than puny Miller City.

Somehow, this small band of warriors had won the day, And if Simpson still wondered if it was all just a dream, all he had to do was glance over his shoulder at the gold trophy on the seat behind him to know that it wasn't.

The shrill scream of sirens suddenly brought Simpson and his fellow passengers upright in their seats. The caravan had reached the Hancock County limits, and a police escort was waiting to greet the returning heroes.

The caravan meandered into Findlay, took a detour down South

Adams Street past Simpson's boyhood home (his parents had been to nearly every game), then headed west on State Route 224.

Another escort, this one made up cruisers and fire trucks from most of the villages in the county, picked up the caravan at the Putnam County line and led the parade into Ottawa. There it was estimated over 8,000 die-hard basketball fans waited to welcome the band of boys who had put not only their own little town, but the basketball-rabid county as a whole on the state map.

Leipsic had advanced to the state tournament in 1925. Ottoville followed in 1937. But that was in the era before regional play, and both had lost their first-round games in the 16-team state tournament format.

Now a county that considered basketball king had a true champion upon the throne, and they wanted an entire state to acknowledge the inauguration.

Simpson, surrounded by his starting five in the borrowed Nash, led the parade. Bringing up the rear was Daisy, Skip's pet cow. Even with the state championship trophy in hand, someone had thought to bring along the bovine reminder of Miller City's rural, small-town roots.

A huge banquet was served at the Eagles' hall. Mayors and superintendents gave speeches. Then they piled back into their cars and renewed the parade, through Glandorf and Leipsic and New Cleveland before finally heading home to Miller City, where another banquet and a huge rally were held in the school's gymnasium.

Finally, when it was all over, Simpson and his players gathered one last time. There were no more basketball games to be played. Every obstacle had been cleared, every challenge had been met. In the building appropriately dubbed "The Barn," they were finally home once again. They had come full circle on one of the most remarkable rides in Ohio prep basketball history.

There is something esoteric in the human spirit, a spark of unbridled hope and boundless optimism that smolders within each and every one of us. It is why we dream and why we strive.

And sometimes, sometimes, that ember becomes a flame that cannot, despite all odds, be extinguished.

During the 1949–50 basketball season, Norris Simpson and his Miller City Wildcats embodied that flame. The littlest team in the state had brought home the biggest trophy. For the rookie head coach who towered above his players and the team whose will to win towered above all others, it was the perfect ending to a perfect season.

TATE PUBLISHING & *Enterprises*

Tate Publishing is committed to excellence in the publishing industry. Our staff of highly trained professionals, including editors, graphic designers, and marketing personnel, work together to produce the very finest books available. The company reflects the philosophy established by the founders, based on Psalms 68:11,

"THE LORD GAVE THE WORD AND GREAT WAS THE COMPANY OF THOSE WHO PUBLISHED IT."

If you would like further information, please call
1.888.361.9473
or visit our website
www.tatepublishing.com

TATE PUBLISHING & *Enterprises*, LLC
127 E. Trade Center Terrace
Mustang, Oklahoma 73064 USA